~Stitch It Up a Notch~
How to Piece *Perfect* Quilts

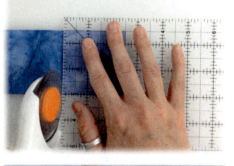
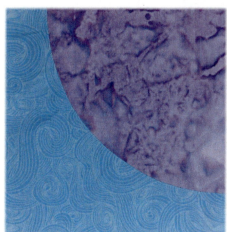
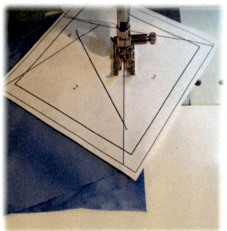
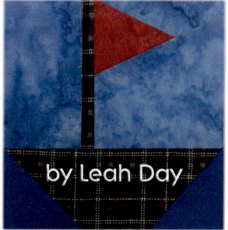

by Leah Day

Publisher: Leah Day / Day Style Designs Inc.

Editor: Janice Brewster / Creative Girlfriends Press

Originally published as a digital ebook and video collection by Day Style Designs Inc,

P.O Box 386, Earl, NC 28152

Email: Support@daystyledesigns.com

www.LeahDay.com

2014 © Leah C Day

All rights reserved. Apart from any fair dealing for the purpose of private study, research, criticism, or review, no part of this publication may be reproduced, stored in a retrieval system, or transmitted in any form or by any means, electronic, electrical, chemical, mechanical, optical, photocopying, recording or otherwise, without the prior written permission of the copyright owner. Inquiries should be addressed to the publisher.

We have taken great care to ensure that the information included in this book is accurate and presented in good faith, but no warranty is provided nor results guaranteed. Having no control over the choices of materials or procedures used, neither the author nor Day Style Designs Inc. shall have any liability to any person or entity with respect to any loss or damage caused directly or indirectly by the information contained in this book.

Any similarities to existing designs, graphics, or patterns is purely coincidental.

This version of Stitch It Up a Notch: How to Piece Perfect Quilts is published by Create Space Direct Publishing.

ISBN-13 - 978-1501000379

ISBN-10 - 1501000373

Table of Contents

Introduction - Page 4

Chapter 1 - Quilting Basics - Page 6

Chapter 2 - Fabric - Page 10

Chapter 3 - Fabric Preparation - Page 17

Chapter 4 - Press, Starch, and Square - Page 23

Chapter 5 - Fabric Cutting - Page 34

Chapter 6 - Basic Machine Piecing - Page 45

Chapter 7 - Chain and Strip Piecing - Page 61

Chapter 8 - Piecing a Quilt Top - Page 71

Chapter 9 - Let's Piece Triangles - Page 86

Chapter 10 - Piecing Weird Shapes - Page 102

Chapter 11 - Paper Piecing for Perfection - Page 115

Conclusion - Page 124

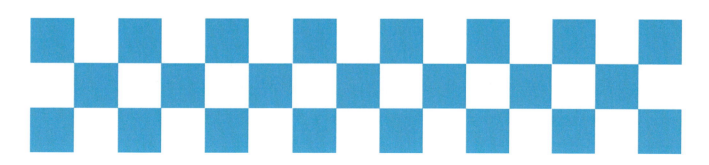

Introduction

What makes a perfectly pieced quilt? Whether it's your seams matching perfectly at every intersection, or the finished blocks measuring exactly the correct size, the ability to work with fabric to create perfect blocks and quilts is a skill worth building.

As you will learn in this guide, proper piecing comes from not just the stitches and seam allowance you use on your sewing machine, but also from the way you prepare and cut your fabric.

Taking the time to learn each skill is very important if you want your blocks to finish perfectly with straight seams and crisp points every time.

All quilters have quilts in their closet that aren't quite right. Whether it's seams not matching up properly or blunt triangle points, imperfect blocks are noticeable, and can be frustrating if you don't understand why mistakes are happening or how to improve.

The picture to the left is a simple hand pieced flower block pieced with small hexagon shapes. As you can see, not all the hexagons are perfectly formed: there are some pleats and puckering in the fabric that throw off the symmetry of this beautiful block.

In the second photo, the block is flipped over and you can see the source of this block's issues: inconsistent seam lines, inconsistent size of the hexagons, and inconsistent pressing of the seam allowances. ***Clearly being inconsistent is a recipe for imperfect quilts!***

It's challenging to piece this block accurately unless you have control over the fabric movement, perfect cutting of the hexagon shapes, and precise stitching to take away the exact ¼ inch seam allowance we use for quilt piecing.

Learning how to piece a block like this perfectly might be more time-consuming and require more steps in the cutting and piecing process than you usually take.

Try to be open minded to these extra steps – yes, you might have used different techniques for years, but it's never too late to try something new!

Accurate piecing is definitely one skill we all must build. While most books on piecing don't seem to go beyond the basics, this guide will challenge you to move beyond piecing simple squares and rectangles and into piecing triangles, curves, and even hexagon shapes with precision and accuracy.

Let's go piece it up a notch!

Leah Day

This book is dedicated to my husband, Josh Day.

Your practical common sense advice has never steered me wrong. Love you baby!

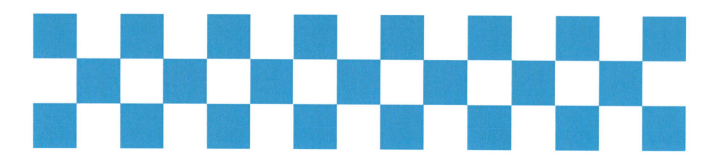

~ Chapter 1 ~
Quilting Basics

When I began quilting in 2005, one of the most annoying aspects of the craft was how much information teachers, book writers, and even the lecturers at my local quilt guild meetings would take for granted.

To a beginner, quilting can be immensely confusing due to the hundreds of little steps and numerous strong opinions this craft has picked up over the years.

This chapter is filled with practical information and explanations on what it takes to make a quilt from the quilt sandwich to the seam allowance that makes quilt piecing possible. We all start at the beginning when it comes to making quilts, and it's best to start with the most basic understanding of what a quilt is, and how this whole process works.

Chapter 1 Sections:

What Is a Quilt? – Page 7

Quilt Blocks - Page 7

Traditional Quilt Components – Page 8

Quilting Math – Page 9

Seam Allowance - Page 9

Helpful Chart of Fraction and Decimal Equivalents - Page 9

What is a Quilt?

The simplest definition of a quilt is three layers of material with quilting stitches running through all 3 layers holding them securely together. The layers of a quilt include:

Quilt top - This top layer can be pieced, appliqued, or even a single piece of fabric. The quilt top contains the major design elements and colors of the quilt.

Batting or wadding - This middle layer determines the warmth, puffiness, and drape of the finished quilt. Thicker or loftier batting will make your quilt warmer.

Fabric backing - This bottom layer forms the back of the quilt, and while it's not a focal point of the quilt itself, it's important to use high-quality fabric because this side gets just as much wear as the quilt top, especially when folded.

These three materials are layered together to create a quilt sandwich. However, simply layering the materials doesn't make a quilt a quilt. In order for a quilt to be a quilt, there must be some form of quilting stitches or tying that holds the layers together securely.

Quilt Blocks

Our focus for this book is the quilt top and how to piece small fabric shapes together perfectly to create beautiful, geometric designs. The easiest way to piece a quilt top is to start with quilt blocks.

A quilt block is a small unit of a quilt top. We can create an infinite variety of quilt blocks using simple shapes like squares, rectangles, triangles, and quarter circles.

Despite the infinite variety of shapes to work with, certain blocks and designs have gained enormous popularity over the years. You may recognize names like Nine Patch and Grandmother's Flower Garden as traditional quilt blocks your grandmother or great-grandmothers might have pieced.

These blocks are both simple and beautiful and offer a connection with the past with every stitch. No matter which blocks you piece, however, the requirement for them all is the same:

To piece these shapes together so the seams match with perfect points and corners, you must learn to piece with both precision and accuracy in every seam.

Traditional Quilt Components

A traditional patchwork quilt is usually comprised of three main elements: blocks, sashing, and borders.

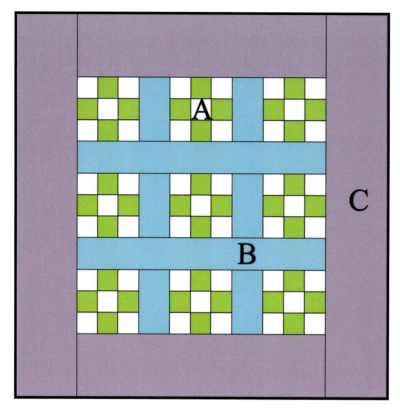

First multiple fabrics are cut into shapes and pieced together into **blocks (A)**.

These blocks are then either pieced together side by side, or sewn to strips of fabric called **sashing (B)**.

Sashing is used to create space between the blocks so they have more visual impact. It can also be used to expand the size of the quilt so fewer blocks need to be pieced.

Finally, longer strips of fabric are pieced around the edges to form a **border (C)**.

The border is used much like the frame around a picture – to enhance and highlight the design within. A border can also be used to expand the size of a quilt so it fits perfectly on your bed.

Within this traditional quilt layout, there are thousands of design variations. By changing the blocks, size of the sashing, width of the borders, you have an infinite opportunity to create new, beautiful quilts in any shape and size you need.

So what determines how this entire puzzle of pieces and shapes fits together?

Math! A super simple rule of addition and subtraction is what creates our beautiful quilt blocks and tops. The rule is this:

Whatever you add, you take away, leaving exactly the shape that will fit.

Quilting Math

Oh no! Math?! How in the world will I learn how to quilt now?!

Yes, all quilts involve simple math, but nothing more complicated than the super simple equation on the right:

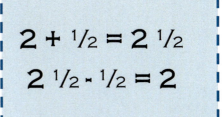

$$2 + 1/2 = 2\ 1/2$$
$$2\ 1/2 - 1/2 = 2$$

Whatever you add, you need to take away exactly.

Seam Allowance

Every time we cut a piece of fabric for quilting, we add a little extra space to all the edges.

This extra fabric is called seam allowance because it literally allows space for the seam to be sewn. As you sew any seam, you aim to take exactly that amount of extra fabric away.

Because quilters are frugal by nature, we want to use a small seam allowance to minimize fabric waste.

In the US, the standard seam allowance is ¼ inch. Special piecing or patchwork presser feet can be found for most machines that will enable you to piece this seam allowance easily and accurately.

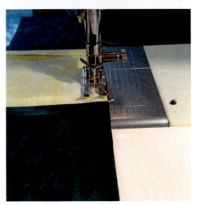

However in many areas of the world where the metric system is the standard unit of measure, a 7.5 mm seam allowance is used for piecing instead.

While it's possible to find rotary rulers and quilt patterns written for the metric system, it's far more common to find patterns written in inches, and designed to use ¼-inch seams to piece the fabrics together.

For the purposes of this book, we learn how to piece our quilts perfectly with an accurate ¼-inch seam allowance. The key to perfectly piecing quilts is mastering the art of adding and subtracting seam allowance for every seam you stitch from the blocks to the sashing to the borders.

Helpful Chart of Fraction and Decimal Equivalents

Fraction	¼	½	¾
Decimal	0.25	0.5	0.75

You will sometimes see a cutting measurement written in fractions like 2 ½ inches. The exact same measurement might be written by another pattern as 2.5 inches.

You should memorize these equivalent measurements so no matter which way a pattern is written, you will understand the measurement being described. All measurements written in this book will be noted using fractions for clarity.

~ Chapter 2~
Fabric

The most important element within a quilt is the fabric used to create it. Not only does fabric cover both sides of the quilt, but the quality and durability of the fabric you choose will determine the longevity of your finished quilt.

Quilts should be made to stand the test of time and frequent use. What is the point of piecing a gorgeous quilt only to keep it folded on a shelf because the fabrics are too delicate for the quilt to be enjoyed by your children or grandchildren?

To make life simple, it's best to use fabrics that can be washed and dried as easily as your clothing. The fussier the fabric, the more frustrating it will be to make your quilt and to care for it once it's finished.

Chapter 2 Sections:

Woven Cotton Fabric – Page 11

Fabric Quality - Page 12

Poor Fabrics Make Impossible Quilts - Page 13

Cotton Alternatives – Page 13

Fabric Anatomy - Page 14

Fabric Terms - Page 16

Woven Cotton Fabric

Generally, 100% woven cotton fabric is the best choice for quilt piecing.

This fabric is now available in an amazing range of colors and prints, including precut fabrics which are collections of color-coordinated fabrics already cut in standard sizes and shapes.

Cotton fabrics like these are easy to find at your local quilt shop or online in thousands of colors and prints, which means you can always find the perfect fabrics for every quilt.

Within the vast world of woven cotton fabric, you may find many new words to describe the color or way the fabric design was prepared. Here's just a few you may find:

Solids - This fabric is very practically named for a very practical fabric. It's a single solid color that usually doesn't have a discernable right or wrong side.

This makes it a great fabric for beginners or anyone with orientation issues. Solids are usually less expensive than prints or batiks, making it a great choice for thrifty quilters.

Prints - This cotton fabric has a pretty printed design, usually on only one side of the fabric. The popularity of quilting and printed cotton fabrics has created a huge surge in the number and variety of prints available.

Prints are also published conveniently in fabric lines, with corresponding designs in matching colors which will make picking multiple fabrics for a project easier.

Print-on-demand prints - The variety of printed fabrics has gotten even bigger in recent years with the addition of print-on-demand services like **Spoonflower.com.**

If you have a specific color or pattern in mind for a special quilt, you can now design it yourself, upload the design to a print-on-demand website, and have custom fabric printed as you need it.

However, this fabric does have specific care requirements that other fabrics don't. You must use only **chlorine-free detergent** and wash the fabrics very gently. Excessive washing, or using the wrong detergent can cause these fabrics to fade faster than regularly printed fabric.

While print-on-demand fabrics are more expensive than regular prints, and have special care requirements, the ability to design your own fabric is both fun and exciting.

Batiks - This high quality cotton fabric is hand dyed with wax to create beautiful designs and the most vivid colors.

Because the fabric is dyed, it usually doesn't have a discernable right or wrong side, similar to solid fabrics. This feature makes these fabrics a great choice for quilters with orientation issues - you'll never make the mistake of piecing fabrics wrong sides together!

Batiks are hand dyed in Indonesia using higher quality, tighter weave cotton fabric. These fabrics not only look different from solid or print fabrics, they also feel different to piece and quilt because of this tighter weave.

It's important to understand that you can use all of these fabrics - solids, batiks, and prints together in one quilt so long as the fabrics are properly prepared for cutting and piecing. Zoom ahead to page 18 to start learning about fabric preparation.

Fabric Quality

Always feel your fabric before you buy it!

Fabric quality is extremely important when it comes to precision piecing. You can utilize all the best tools and techniques, but if the fabric is low quality to start, the finished quilt will be low quality as well. When buying fabric, go to a fabric store so you can feel the fabrics.

Run the material through your fingers – does it feel soft or rough? Does it feel loose and weak? Can you see through the fabric easily? If you tug on it, does it stretch out of shape?

To make a quality quilt, the best choice is to find a cotton fabric that has a tight weave and solidly printed or dyed surface. Watch out for fabrics that are extremely loose and stretchy feeling.

Especially look for gaps or splits in the weave of the fabric and distortion of the printed pattern.

Fabric distortion is normal along ripped edges

If you rip fabric to length, you will always see a little distortion along the ripped edge as you see in the photo on the left. When you trim the fabric square (page 37) you'll need to make sure to cut off at least ½ inch of fabric along the edge to remove all this distortion.

Looser weave, thinner cotton fabrics are nice enough for sewing garments, but they usually can't take the wear and tear required by a utilitarian bed quilt. The looser the weave, the more likely a fabric will stretch and distort as well, making it an absolute nightmare to control while cutting and piecing.

Certainly beware of bargain-bin fabrics. The price may be appealing, but you really won't get much bang for your buck because your finished quilt is only as good as the materials that go into it.

Poor Fabrics Make Impossible Quilts

Leah's Note - *I made the mistake of choosing bargain-bin white and pink cotton fabric for one of my first quilts. These fabrics were so thin, you could easily see your hand through the material.*

As soon as the quilt was pieced, I knew I'd made a big mistake. I kept wondering - how can I layer this with any batting without the fibers showing or pulling through the fabric?

I also feared the quilt would quickly wear out with use. So this cute pink baby quilt pieced over nine years ago has remained an unfinished project in my closet.

I can't throw it away because it was one of my first quilts, but I also can't finish it because what is the point of finishing something so fragile?

I hope you don't make the same mistake because projects like this are no fun!

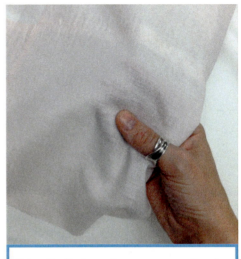

It's a bad sign when you can clearly see through your fabric!

Cotton Alternatives

Cotton blends - Checking at your local big box discount store, you're likely to run into woven cotton blends that look a lot like the 100% cotton fabrics, but they are significantly cheaper.

These fabrics are usually cotton / polyester blends, and yes, in a pinch they can work for quilt piecing; however, these fabrics can be very unpredictable when it comes time to layer and quilt your quilt top.

Just be sure to **feel the fabric before purchasing** – if it's rough and scratchy in the store, chances are it will feel far worse in your finished quilt.

Bed sheets - Maybe it has something to do with our scrap-saving nature, but quilting and frugality seem to run hand in hand.

It certainly makes sense to look for the largest amount of fabric you can get for the least amount of cost. 100% cotton bed sheets might be an option to look into if you can find a color and style you like.

Working with a bed-sheet sized piece of fabric can be challenging when it comes to fabric preparation. Take your time cutting down the large piece of fabric into smaller, more manageable pieces so you can easily press and square the fabric accurately before cutting.

One other note about bed sheets – make sure to pick a color you like as a large sheet will make many quilts and many scraps and it may eventually feel like you'll never use all that fabric up!

Fabric Anatomy

As we learn how to prepare fabric, it's important to understand what features you can expect to see in every yard you buy.

When your fabric was created, it was woven on a loom, with **warp threads** pulled tight to form the length of the fabric. **Weft threads** were woven up and down between the warp threads from side to side to lock the fibers together.

These perpendicular threads form every inch of every square of fabric you own, and they create the structure and stability of all woven cotton fabric.

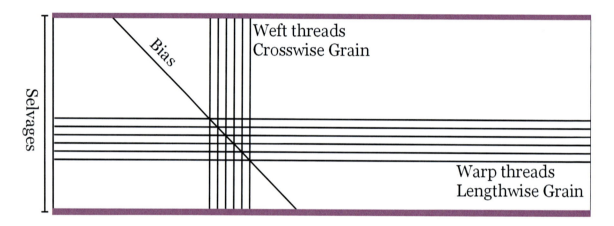

In finished fabric, the straight lines created by the warp and weft threads are called grain lines.

Lengthwise grain – These threads run down the length of the fabric, parallel with the selvage edges. There's usually very little stretch in lengthwise grain because these threads were pulled so tightly on the loom when the fabric was woven.

The bias is a stretchy direction so be gentle handling pieces that involve this angle

Crosswise grain – These threads run perpendicular to the lengthwise grain, so selvage to selvage, or across the width (usually 42 inches) of the fabric.

Crosswise grain has a little more stretch because this thread was woven up and down between the lengthwise warp fibers and less tension was put on these threads during the manufacturing process.

Woven fabric does have one stretchy direction – **the bias**. The bias runs diagonally across both grain lines and is the stretchiest direction of woven cotton fabric.

The reason this angle is stretchy is because it crosses the fabric grain lines on the diagonal. When you tug fabric in this direction, you can easily create gaps between the woven threads which allow for more stretch in the fabric.

Why is grain line so important?

When you cut a piece of fabric, you're slicing across threads that build a stable structure. Every cut into a piece of fabric weakens it in a small way.

Don't worry – fabric is designed to be cut, but it's important to understand that there are two ways to cut fabric and one is far more stable and predictable than the other.

On-grain – When you cut a piece of fabric and your slice runs perfectly parallel and perpendicular with the grain line, your cut is on-grain.

This type of cut is more stable because the woven fibers are still locked together in that perfect, woven arrangement right to the very edges of the cut shape.

This cut is also "square" to the grain lines because they run at 90-degree angles to your cut. Your goal is always to cut square to the grain lines of your fabric.

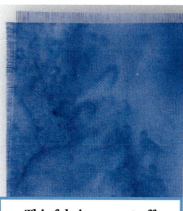

This fabric was cut parallel with the grain lines

Off-grain – When you cut fabric and your slice runs randomly over the surface of the grain line, you've made an off-grain cut. This piece is going to be far more unstable, especially along the edges, which may begin to fray immediately.

When you cut off-grain, you introduce a little taste of the bias – not the true bias, the stretchiest part of the fabric, but a small amount of diagonal direction into the cut edge.

This allows more stretch into that cut edge, making it more likely to "grow" and stretch out as you piece it to other pieces rather than staying the stable shape you cut.

One key to perfect piecing is always respecting the grain lines of your woven cotton fabric. We'll get back to grain line in Chapter 4 when we learn how to square our fabric for cutting.

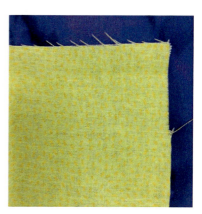

This fabric was cut off grain so the edge will unravel at an angle

Signs of off-grain cutting

You can easily see when fabric pieces are cut off-grain because they will naturally being to fray immediately at the edges. The stray threads will also pull off at an angle to the cut shape, which can make precision piecing practically impossible.

If you notice your pieces fraying along the edges, give the threads a tug and take a look at the angle the grain line runs through the piece. How far out of grain is your cut piece? If it's badly out of whack, it might be a good idea to stop and cut a new piece that will work more predictably in your quilt.

Fabric Terms

Now that we know a bit about fabric anatomy, let's tackle some common terms you will see to describe the cotton fabric most quilters use.

Fabric width – Most 100% cotton woven fabric will measure 42 – 44 inches wide. You can also find 60 inch wide fabrics which will cost a little more per yard because you're getting more fabric for every yard. You can also find 108 inch super wide fabrics which are used as quilt backings.

Selvage – The edges of the fabric are always a little denser weave and usually printed with some information like the brand, designer, and color test. For dyed or batik fabrics, there will be no printing, but the edge will feel slightly stiffer. This edge is created in the weaving process to keep the fabric square on the loom.

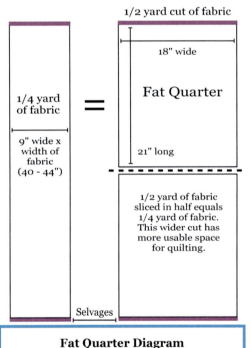

Fat Quarter Diagram

Selvage to selvage - This is referring to the space between the selvages, or the width of the fabric. So a "selvage to selvage cut" means slicing fabric from the selvage on one side straight across to the selvage on the opposite side, which is the most common way fabric is cut.

Cut edge – This is the edge of the fabric that was cut in the store. Typically this runs from selvage to selvage across the fabric.

Yardage – Fabric purchased in the US is typically sold in yards – 36 inches of length. In other areas of the world where the metric system is used, fabric is sold in meters, which is equivalent to 39.4 inches.

Fat quarter – A fat quarter is a cut of fabric used exclusively for quilting.

A typical ¼-yard cut would be a 9-inch strip of 42 inch wide fabric, which is very narrow and can be tricky to work with.

A fat quarter fixes this issue by cutting the same amount of fabric in a different way.

First cut ½ yard of fabric, then slice that piece in half to create two ¼-yard pieces.

These are called fat quarters because they offer the same surface area as a ¼-yard cut, but are now "fat" – measuring usually 18 by 21 inches.

Fat quarters can be easily found in most quilt shops from $3 - $5, which makes them a fun cut of fabric to collect!

~ Chapter 3 ~
Fabric Preparation

When you bring home fabric from the store, do you know where it's been? Do you know what chemicals were used to create it? Do you have any idea how it will behave during cutting, piecing, or in your finished quilt?

The answer to all of these questions is no – when we purchase fabric from stores, we know very little about it other than we love the color or print.

At this point the fabric is rather unpredictable, which is definitely not what you want for perfect piecing. To cut and piece precisely, you need control over every aspect of the process, and that starts by properly preparing your fabric before a single cut is made.

Chapter 3 Sections:

Prewashing Your Fabric - Page 18

Leah's Prewashing Story - Page 19

Build a Prewashing Habit - Page 20

We've Got a Bleeder! - Page 21

When Prewashing Is Impossible - Page 22

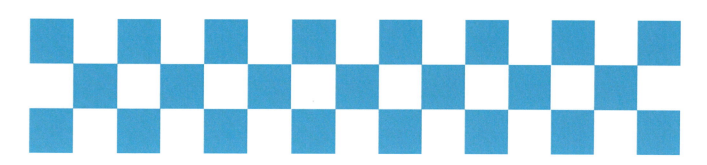

Prewashing Your Fabric

Proper fabric preparation marks the beginning of any quilting project. This is the step where you wash, dry, iron, and then starch your fabric to make it ready to cut and piece.

This is usually the part that most people skip. There are three main opinions on prewashing and ironing fabric before cutting and quilting.

Opinion #1 - Prewashing is a waste of time.

Opinion #2 - Prewashing is absolutely essential to the success of your quilt.

Opinion #3 - What? I didn't know I was supposed to wash my fabric first!

You can see how the quilting world is split into two camps:

Quilters who prewash vs. quilters who don't

This is an understandable divide. Whether you never knew to prewash your fabric, or you were told by another quilting friend or teacher that it was unnecessary, many quilters these days just don't think it's important to wash fabric before cutting and piecing.

This is an easy step to skip because it seems so unnecessary. When we buy fabric at a store, it's crisp and smooth. Chemicals used in the manufacturing process make the fabric stiffer, which makes it easier to handle when cutting and piecing.

So it seems an easy decision to not prewash fabric, which takes extra time to wash, dry, and then press the fabric to remove wrinkles. And then what if you have to STARCH the fabric? Who has time for all that?

Yes, it's an understandable choice to make, but now let's look at this from the predictability angle. In order to piece perfectly, we really want to work with fabric that will act as predictably as possible, that we can cut easily, and will piece together with ease.

If you purchase two fabrics from a shop, do you know what chemicals were used to manufacture them? Do you know if they both have the same amount of sizing or stiffness on the surface? Do you know if the fold in the middle of the fabric is actually square with the grain lines of the fabric?

The answer to all of these questions is no. Any two fabrics you buy from a quilt shop could have different chemicals, different amounts of stretch and give, and most likely both fabrics will have heavily creased, selvage-to-selvage folds that are not square to the grain lines of the fabric.

In short – these fabrics are very unpredictable!

Prewashing prepares fabric in the following ways:

1. Removes chemicals from the manufacturing process which might make one fabric super stiff, but another fabric very loose. All your fabric needs to have the same universal stiffness.

2. Removes the embedded fold which is hardly ever square to the grain line of fabric. Now you will be able to fold the fabric square and cut strips perfectly on-grain.

3. Removes any excess dyes from the fabric, which could potentially ruin a beautiful quilt by leaking from one color to another.

4. Relaxes and preshrinks the fabric. Without this preshrink, your finished quilt will always shrink and crinkle on the surface, which is pretty for certain styles of bed quilts, but not appropriate for art quilts or wall hangings.

Prewashing removes the embedded fold in fabric so it can be cut accurately

Ultimately, by washing the fabric first, you will have far more control over how your finished quilt will look.

Leah's Prewashing Story

I started my quilting life as an avid non-prewasher. I lived in an apartment and washing anything meant a trip to the laundromat. For the first three years that I quilted, I never prewashed any fabric at all. EVER.

And then one day I took a hard look at my quilts and realized they just weren't looking that good. I had bought into the idea that it was okay not to wash my fabric, but this made me always hesitant to wash my finished quilts. This anxiety lead me to also feel nervous about using and enjoying them – *what if they get dirty? I don't think I can wash them...*

When I finally built up the nerve to throw my first quilt in the wash, I watched in horror as blue dye migrated into the white fabric border.

Leah's First Quilt

I also noticed many odd creases in my fabric that I couldn't get out in the construction process, which were still glaringly obvious in the finished quilt. This was the center crease line where fabric is folded in half and rolled on a bolt, and it's almost impossible to remove without getting the fabric wet.

As I learned more about quilting, I found that that most professional quilters prewash their fabric. Washing the fabric before cutting removes much of the unpredictability from this material and creates smooth, flat quilts that look as good hanging on a wall as they do on a bed.

Since 2008, I've prewashed all fabric before cutting and never had a cause to regret taking a little extra time to ensure every quilt finishes exactly the way I want it to look.

Blue and red fabrics are especially prone to bleed

Build a Prewashing Habit

Prewashing your fabric can certainly feel like a chore to complete before the fun can begin. Most of us purchase fabric and take it straight to our stash, ready and waiting for the next opportunity to sew.

But then the extra time appears and you begin pulling out materials and you're faced with a dilemma – you have this special allotted time to cut, piece, and play, but your fabric isn't ready to go! It needs to be washed and dried, and this process is going to waste all your creative time.

It's easy to see why so many quilters skip this important step due to a combination of lack of time and quilting impulse. However, if properly incorporated into your life with your natural routines and habits, this step will become as easy as tying your shoelaces and brushing your teeth.

The solution here is simple: Have your fabric ready to go, already prewashed and prepared, so you can cut and piece anytime.

Easy Prewashing Routine:

1. Purchase new fabric - Quick! Go now while you have an excuse to buy a lot of new fabric! It's part of the directions!

2. Wash it - Bring your new fabric stash home, sort it by color, and throw it straight in the wash. Make sure to use perfume and dye-free detergent so the fabric will not have a strong scent. Also avoid fabric softeners because we want the fabric to be stiff and easy to work with during cutting and piecing.

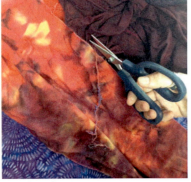

3. Snip, shake, and snap - After washing, shake the fabric out and snip any strings tying the fabric together. If your fabric has wadded itself into a knot, carefully unpick it and shake it out to remove the wrinkles before drying.

Also give the fabric a little snap by holding onto two corners and quickly shaking it in a downward motion. You can hear a "Snap!" sound as the fabric straightens itself back out and most wrinkles disappear.

4. Dry lightly - Throw your fabric in the dryer, but make sure to take it out right at the end of the drying cycle. This ensures the fabric will be fluffy and smooth.

The longer the fabric stays in the dryer, the more likely it will form deep wrinkles that take more effort and time to remove.

5. Put it away wrinkled - Fold the fabric and add it to your stash wrinkled. Now whenever you're ready to cut and piece a quilt, all you have to do is pull the fabrics and press the amounts you need to work with.

Why put away fabric wrinkled?

Don't we have to start the dreaded chore of ironing immediately after fabric is washed?

It's a waste of time to press fabric that isn't going to be immediately used. If you store fabric folded, the folds will cause creases in the fabric that will need to be pressed out again, doubling your efforts.

It makes more sense to store fabric wrinkled. It has been washed and dried, but not pressed so no effort or time is wasted in the process.

It's also better for fabric to be stored completely clean, with no starch or sizing on the surface which could attract moths.

Using this method, you will build a habit for pre-washing that will take no time away from piecing your next project, and ensure you have perfectly prewashed fabric for every project in the future.

We've got a Bleeder!

When washing your fabric, make sure to sort by color and try not to mix very dark colors with very light.

One way to help reduce the amount of migrating dye in your washer is to use a **Color Catcher** or **Dye Grabber**. These products are available in the laundry aisle in grocery stores in the U.S. and come as either disposable sheets, or a reusable cloth that you throw into the top of the wash at the beginning of the load.

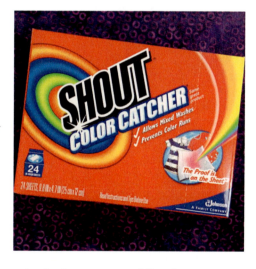

Color catchers work by using a dye fixative chemical, like soda ash, to attract loose dyes in the water and bind them to the disposable sheet.

White square test - Hand dyed and batik fabrics can be particularly prone to bleeding. In addition to a Color Catcher, you should also throw a small 6 – 10-inch square of white fabric in with a load of these fabrics.

The white fabric will also absorb any excess dyes in the water, and provide a solid visual on how much dye is migrating and how much power it has to darken or discolor other fabrics.

At the end of the wash if this white square has changed color, you'll know at least one of the fabrics in that batch is bleeding dye, and you should run that load again.

Continue to wash that load of fabric with a color catcher and fresh white scrap of fabric until the white fabric comes out of the wash perfectly white with no trace of discoloration. At that point, you will know with visual proof that the excess dye has been washed away, leaving only color-safe fabric behind.

When Prewashing is Impossible

If you haven't had a habit for prewashing fabric, and you've been making quilts for years, chances are you have a very big scrap stash accumulated that's filled with unwashed fabric.

Unfortunately scraps smaller than 12 inches are usually too small to wash. You can certainly try washing them in a small garment bag, but chances are the scraps will just tie themselves into a big, messy knot in your washing machine.

What to do with unwashed scraps - piece all of them up into a scrappy quilt to empty your scrap bin before the new, prewashed scraps get tossed in on top. Find instructions for cutting shapes from scrap fabric on page 44.

As you begin prewashing your fabric, the new scraps from prewashed fabrics will behave a lot more predictably and can be cut and pieced perfectly into any type of quilt. It's a good idea to keep washed and unwashed scraps separated because there will always be a chance that loose dyes in the unwashed fabric will bleed over the finished quilt.

Precut fabrics are also too small to be prewashed.

Precut packs of 2 ½-inch strips, 10-inch squares, 5-inch squares, and even hexagon shapes are just too small to wash as the fabric itself could be badly distorted as it goes through the washer and dryer.

In this situation, you just have to cross your fingers! It's really a gamble with precut fabrics because you never know if the fabric will bleed, or leak excess dye across the surface of your finished quilt.

These precuts are a bit risky in many ways because not all pieces will be cut properly on-grain. If you find yourself struggling to piece with precuts accurately, try cutting fresh yardage to see if it's actually the inaccuracy of the precut fabric that is to blame.

It's also important to remember that precut fabrics will not retain their smooth, flat shape after piecing because of the inherent shrinkage that will occur as the cotton fabric is washed and the fibers relax. Any quilt pieced with unwashed fabric will shrink slightly to form a slightly crinkly, wrinkled appearance across the surface of the quilt.

For the best results, take the time to starch and press your precut pieces to make them stiffer and more predictable to piece. Even though precut fabrics can save time in the fabric selection and cutting process, they will still require a little time and effort in order to piece perfectly.

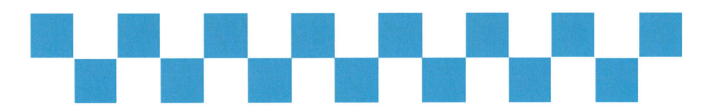

~ Chapter 4~
Press, Starch, and Square

At this point your fabric has been prewashed, it's free of loose dyes, and has shrunk slightly to have a relaxed, softer feel. The bad news is in this current state your fabric would be nearly impossible to piece perfectly.

In this chapter we will learn how to regain control over our fabric by bringing back that stiff, stable feel it had when purchased. We create this effect by using starch, which stiffens fabric, and either reduces or eliminates all the stretch and give in the weave.

By stiffening all the fabric in a particular project with the same amount of starch, it will all work identically, which means the process of piecing, matching seams, and stitching accurately will be much, much easier.

Chapter 4 Sections:

Materials Needed for Fabric Preparation - Page 24

Starch Myths and Misuse - Page 25

Starch Alternatives - Page 25

How to Build a Hard Pressing Board - Page 26

How to Starch and Iron Fabric - Page 27

When to Use a Double Layer of Starch - Page 28

Preparing Fabric for Cutting - Page 29

Squaring Your Fabric - Page 30

Squaring Fabric with Two Folds - Page 32

Correcting Skewed Fabric - Page 33

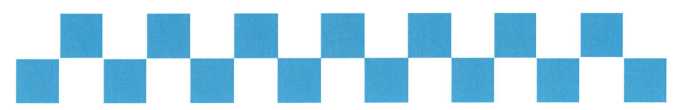

Materials Needed for Fabric Preparation

Really Hot Iron

When starching fabric, a hot, dry iron is best to heat and dry the starch quickly.

If you like to work with steam, try keeping two irons – one filled with water for steaming fabric, and the other with no water for hot, dry work. You may find the hot, dry iron lasts much longer and stays reliably hotter than the steam iron.

Water is the culprit behind steam irons going bad so quickly. If you keep the water out of the iron, it will likely last forever!

Really Hard Pressing Board

Notice this isn't called an "ironing board" which is usually a metal frame covered with a soft, squishy cover. This type of ironing board is really unhelpful as the shifting, plush fabric surface will encourage your fabric to distort as you press.

A pressing board is a much firmer, hard surface that allows you to press the fabric flat without distortion.

Pressing boards are not usually found in stores, but they are very easy to build for yourself out of simple materials. Find instructions on building your hard pressing board on page 26.

Spray Starch

Starch is a natural chemical carbohydrate from plants that we use to stiffen fabric. By making fabric stiffer, we're reducing the stretch and movement in the fabric, which makes it easier to cut and piece accurately.

Starching is an effective weapon in our fight against fabric unpredictability. By making all our fabric equally stiff with a layer of spray starch, we're regaining control and ensuring the pieces come together perfectly.

Look for spray starch at your local grocery store in the laundry aisle. Try to find it in a spray bottle, like this **Niagara brand spray starch,** rather than an aerosol can. Spray bottles are better for the environment, and it's also easier to tell how much liquid is in the bottle so you're less likely to run out unexpectedly.

If you can't find this starch in the spray bottles, you can always mix your own using pure liquid starch, or starch flakes and water. Make sure to mix it to the right consistency and store your starch according to the package directions.

Starch Myths and Misuse

Starch has gotten a bad reputation in recent years because it is a food-based chemical and can attract moths and other insects, which eat fabric.

Do keep in mind that starch has been used for hundreds of years to stiffen fabric for both clothing and textile production. ***As you wash your fabric, or your finished quilt, you remove the starch from the material completely.***

So if you use starch to stiffen your fabric, cut it, piece it into a quilt, then wash the finished quilt, no starch will remain in the fabric or quilt to attract moths.

Many quilters also dislike starch because of the flaky residue it can leave on fabric or on the soleplate of your iron.

If you follow the directions on page 27 for massaging and flipping your fabric after spraying, the starch will properly bond with the fabric and not flake off. Let's learn how to use this product properly and see the difference it makes for cutting and piecing perfect quilts!

Starch Alternative

If you truly despise the idea of starch, are allergic to it, or simply hate the smell, you might consider mixing up a starch alternative for yourself.

Starch alternative is made with potato vodka, which still has some of the stiffening powers of starch, but with the added bonus of alcohol which quickly burns off, leaving fabric wrinkle-free and crisp.

Starch alternative recipe:

8 ounces (1 cup) filtered water

1 ounce (1 shot) of potato vodka like Luksusowa

Pour the water and vodka into a spray bottle and shake well. Spray onto the fabric using the same directions on page 27.

Leah's Note - *I tried this starch alternative recipe and found it provided no noticeable stiffness or stability to the fabric, so I don't personally recommend it for fabric preparation.*

I also compared this recipe against **Mary Ellen's Best Press** *– a product sold in quilt shops that claims to be "starch and sizing in one." While the fabric was slightly crisper than the homemade recipe, it still did not produce the desired stiffness and stability of regular spray starch. This sizing product cost $9.99, which is very expensive considering a regular bottle of spray starch at my local grocery store costs less than $2 per bottle.*

Again, the point of starch is to stiffen fabric, to reduce all stretch and pliability so it's easy to cut accurately and piece together precisely. Without starch to stiffen the fabric, it will remain unpredictable and impossible to piece perfectly. Try it for yourself and compare these many options open to you. Ultimately stiffer fabric is our goal because stiffer fabric is predictable and easy to control.

How to Build a Hard Pressing Board

I've used this method to build multiple boards of all shapes and sizes for my sewing room. The key is using cotton canvas which will grip your fabric as you press and prevent it from stretching out of shape as you iron.

Materials

Plywood Board – Look for ½ inch plywood with a smooth finish. Most hardware stores wil cut down large pieces for you in the store.

Thin 100% cotton batting - Quilter's Dream Cotton in the select thickness is my favorite choice.

Cotton canvas fabric

Staples in a staple gun and a hammer to pound in reluctant staples

Directions

1. Prepare your plywood by cutting it into the size you want. Rectangles measuring approximately 24 by 48 inches are a nice size because the width of fabric can be stretched across the surface and still leave space for your iron to rest.

2. Using the board as a template, cut a piece of cotton canvas 4 inches larger than the board on all sides. Cut a piece of cotton batting 2 inches larger than the board on all sides.

3. Place the cotton batting on the board and smooth into place. Holding the batting in place, flip the board over and smooth the batting around the edges of the board to the back side, carefully folding the corners to reduce bulk. Staple into place on the back of the board.

4. Flip the board over and center the cotton canvas on top. Smooth over the surface just as you did with the batting. Holding the canvas in place, flip the board over and smooth the canvas around the edges of the board to the back side, carefully folding the corners to reduce bulk.

5. Starting in the middle of the top edge, fold the cotton canvas to the wrong side of the board and staple into place. Secure the entire edge into place with staples spaced every 2-4 inches apart.

6. Now repeat with the bottom edge – pull the canvas around to the back of the board, stretching the fabric tight and staple to secure.

7. Now pull the canvas on the left side to the back side of the board and staple into place.

8. Repeat with the right side – pull the canvas around to the back of the board, stretching the fabric tight and staple to secure.

9. Hammer in any reluctant staples with a hammer. Then cover the wrong side of the board by gluing a piece of craft felt over the staples and wood to protect your table top.

How to Starch and Iron Fabric

1. Rip to smaller sizes – We've already prewashed the fabric according to the directions in Chapter 3. If you've purchased several yards at a time, it's a good idea to break this large amount of yardage down into manageable 1-yard lengths.

I like to snip the selvage edge of the fabric and rip a 1-yard section to fit on my pressing board. Ripping fabric yardage like this is a quick way to break large amounts of fabric up, and a ripped edge will be automatically on grain, though a bit frayed and loose where the fibers were stressed.

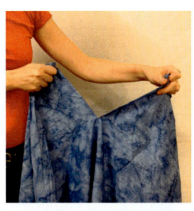

> **Leah's Note** - *For fabric pieces smaller than ½ yard, and especially any form of strip cutting, I cut with a rotary cutter instead of ripping so I lose less fabric and keep a clean edge.*

2. Spray starch – Spread the fabric **right side up** over the surface of your pressing board and spray evenly with starch.

If the fabric extends beyond the pressing board, shift the fabric off the front of the board and continue to spray each section until the entire right side of the fabric is entirely coated with starch.

3. Massage the starch in - Now flip the fabric over, bunch it up into a log and give the fabric a gentle massage. Be gentle when handling your fabric now as it can easily distort when wet.

The purpose of this gentle massage is to encourage the starch to bond with the fibers in your fabric, rather than on your iron or your pressing board.

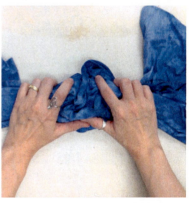

4. Flip fabric - Now flip the fabric **right side down** on the pressing board and gently reposition it over the surface.

By flipping the fabric over, you're guaranteeing that the starch bonds to the fabric and will not flake off on your iron.

5. Press the fabric dry – Now press the fabric with a hot, dry iron. Press lightly first to slightly dry the fabric, then press again to totally dry the starch and bond it to the fabric. Be careful not to pull your iron hard against the wet fabric, as it can easily distort.

Watch out when pressing a light color fabric in particular as it can scorch if you apply excessive heat to one spot.

Your finished fabric should feel noticeably stiff and dry to the touch. If any areas are slightly damp, press again until totally dry.

When to Use a Double Layer of Starch

For most techniques, one layer of starch will sufficiently stiffen the fabric to make it easy to handle and piece predictably.

However, for certain special techniques, especially any piecing techniques involving bias - the naturally stretchiest direction of fabric - it's a good idea to starch the fabric on both the front and back side so it's super stiff.

Simply repeat the same steps, this time spraying the wrong side of the fabric, scrunching it up into a log to give it a massage, then flipping it over and spreading it out right side up to press.

Two layers of starch will usually result in super stiff fabric and it will be easy to control even for the toughest techniques. But don't worry, this effect will go away completely after the quilt has been washed.

Starch your fabric two times when...

Piecing blocks that involve bias

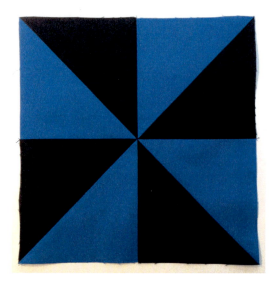

Piecing bias binding

Piecing miniature blocks

Cutting and piecing curves

PREPARING FABRIC FOR CUTTING

You're nearly ready to start cutting this fabric into strips and pieces for your quilt, but there's one super important step that ensures your fabric pieces will be cut on-grain, or square to the lengthwise and crosswise grain lines of the fabric.

If you remember on page 14, we discussed grain line and the difficulty of working with fabrics that are cut off-grain. The photo below showcases exactly what can happen when the fabrics are cut improperly.

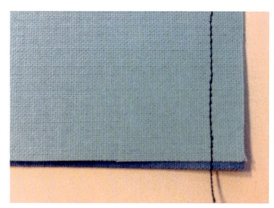

In this situation **the top fabric was cut on-grain**. The square was cut accurately so the lines of threads that make up the fabric were cut parallel with the edges of the square shape.

The bottom fabric was cut off-grain, so the threads that make up the fabric were not running parallel, but at a weird angle to the edges of the square. Because of this angle, this off-grain piece has far more stretch than the top fabric.

These two pieces are going to react differently when fed through the machine. The bottom fabric will be far more likely to stretch out, while the top fabric will likely retain its stable, square shape.

When pieced together, the bottom fabric also comes in contact with the machine's **feed dogs** – the little teeth that feed fabric forward under the presser foot. These little teeth will also contribute to pulling the bottom fabric, which may introduce even more stretch as the pieces are fed through the machine.

Feed dogs are the moving metal teeth under your presser foot

Have you ever pieced two squares together and watched as one "grew" before your eyes? Chances are, this is the reason why – it was not cut square to the grain lines of the fabric and as it was stitched and pulled against the feed dogs, the extra stretch caused the fabric to elongate.

So how do we stop this from happening? How do we ensure that every piece we cut is on-grain and square to the edges of the cut pieces we're working with?

We need to learn how to establish a fold in the fabric we can trust which is square to the grain lines of the fabric. We also need to be able to check ourselves easily so we can maintain this proper alignment as we cut multiple strips and pieces from any large piece of fabric. This might sound tedious or time-consuming, but don't worry! It's actually very easy!

SQUARING YOUR FABRIC

Step 1: Fold - Fold your fabric in half, selvage to selvage.

DO NOT CREASE THIS FOLD.

This is much easier if you work with 1-yard cuts or less. If you have several yards of fabric, cut off pieces no longer than 40 inches to work with.

Step 2: Get a grip on the corners - Hold the fabric up by the ends in front of you. Pinch the corners closest to you with your thumb and index finger. Pinch the corners furthest from you with the other side of your index finger and middle finger.

Step 3: Fabric dance - With the fabric corners held like so, wiggle the fabric back and forth, watching the bottom fold line and the surface of the fabric. When off-grain and out of square, the fabric will not hang properly. It will have ripples and the bottom fold will pull up diagonally to one side.

Both of these fabric are out of square:

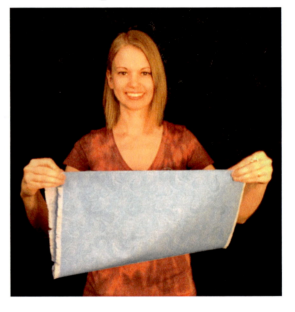

See how the fabric forms a diagonal ripple when held out of square? Also the bottom edge pulls forward at an angle. Keep your eyes peeled for these signs as you wiggle your fabric from side to side.

Remember to keep your hands the same distance from the floor as you do the fabric dance and take your time. It's a skill that gets easier the more often you do it.

So what exactly are we doing as we wiggle our fabric?

By doing this "fabric dance," you will eventually find the happy place in the middle where your fabric hangs straight and flat with no ripples. At this point the threads that run selvage to selvage will be hanging straight through the fold in the fabric. The lengthwise threads will also be running parallel with this fold so both lines are said to be "square" to that fold.

While it may sound like a lot to think about, really it's as simple as holding up the fabric and wiggling it until the bottom hangs straight across with no major diagonal ripples running across the surface.

This fabric is properly square:

When you feel like you've found the spot where the fabric hangs square and straight, lay the fabric down on your cutting mat carefully and run your hands along the fold line.

Step 4: Gently hand press the fold into place, so it forms a straight line across the bottom of your mat.

This bottom fold line is very important and is really a major key to cutting fabric accurately. The whole point of this squaring process is to achieve this perfect fold which is square to the lengthwise and crosswise grain of the fabric.

However, **DO NOT IRON THIS FOLD LINE.**

As you cut, your fabric may slip out of grain - the ruler may shift, the fold may go wonky and suddenly the grain lines of the fabric are no longer square with that fold. You will need to pick up your fabric and wiggle it to square again. Pressing in the fold will just create more work trying to get it out later.

If you're cutting a fat quarter, then one fold will probably be perfect for the size of your mat, but if your fabric is the full 40 to 44 inches wide, you'll need to square a second fold to make it easier to cut.

SQUARING FABRIC WITH TWO FOLDS

1. Start by folding your fabric in half with the selvages together. Do the fabric dance until the fabric is hanging flat and straight. Crease this first fold line gently with your hands.

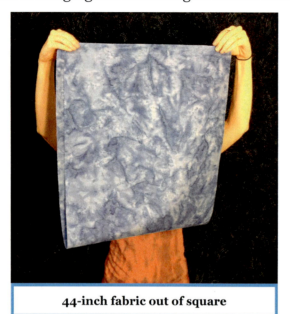

44-inch fabric out of square

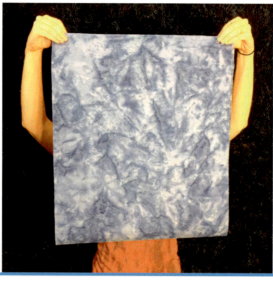

44-inch fabric squared with the grain lines

2. Next, pick up the fabric again only this time with the fold corners in between your thumb and index finger and the two other corners in between your index and middle finger.

3. Do the fabric dance again until this second fold line is hanging straight and flat, then lay it down and gently press this second fold line with your hands.

At first, it may feel a bit more clunky and clumsy squaring the double fold. Take your time and practice this technique. It's worth taking a little extra time and effort to ensure you are folding the fabric properly.

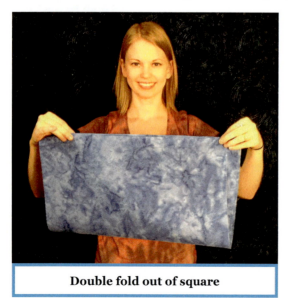

Double fold out of square

Squared double fold

Why aren't the edges matching up?

When your fabric was cut at the store, it was probably cut using the embedded fold line as a guide for the cut. As we've learned, that embedded fold is very rarely square to the grain line of the fabric, so the cut made at the store was most likely very off-grain.

As you square your fabric using the fabric dance, you will be able to see clearly just how off grain your fabrics were cut. You may need to trim off an inch or more of fabric from the edge in order to true up all layers perfectly to the grain line.

Be mindful of this issue when purchasing fabric that is cut to length. Take a close look at the edges of a bolt and look for excessive fraying, which is a sign the fabric is cut off-grain. If your store offers it, ask for an extra 1/16 of a yard added to your fabric amount. This extra 2-inch strip should make up for any fabric you lose as you square up the edges.

CORRECTING SKEWED FABRIC

If your fabric was ripped to length instead of cut, the raw edges should align after the fabric dance because fabric will rip along the crosswise grain. If the edges are not in alignment, your fabric may be skewed, which means the lengthwise and crosswise threads have been tugged out of their normal perpendicular position. Instead of a rectangle, the skewed fabric is actually shaped more like the parallelogram you see on the right.

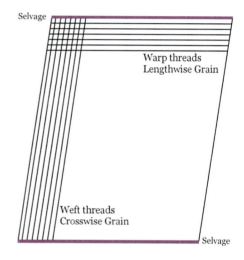

To correct skewed fabric, gently tug on the corners opposite the skewed direction. In the case of the diagram on the right, you would tug on the upper left and bottom right corners.

With a gentle tug, you can encourage the grain lines back into the correct position and return the fabric back to square. Do the fabric dance once more, and check the edges. Repeat this process of gently tugging, dancing, and checking until you find the edges align perfectly.

Skewed fabric edge

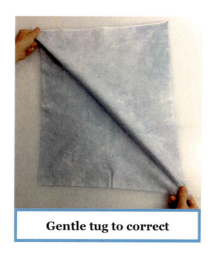

Gentle tug to correct

Fabric in better alignment

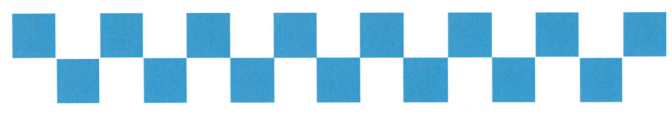

~ Chapter 5 ~
Fabric Cutting

Cutting fabric always makes me smile as I think back to my original opinion about quilting:

"Why bother cutting fabric up just to put it all back together again?"

The fact is, quilting is much more than just cutting up fabric to make a blanket. It's a step-by-step process. It's a journey to creating an object that will do more than just warm your bed. It will bring beauty to your home and love to your children or grandchildren who inherit it. Simply put... a quilt is just a marvel.

But yes, we do cut up large pieces of fabric into smaller pieces, then sew the pieces back together again to make a quilt top. The thing to realize is that all those different fabrics coming together is what makes the magic of any quilt.

Chapter 5 Sections:

Materials Needed for Fabric Cutting - Page 35

Directions for Fabric Cutting - Page 37

Cutting Strips Perfectly - Page 38

Measuring Correctly - Page 39

Lost Thread Calculation - Page 39

One to Rule Them All - Page 40

Cutting Straight Strips - Page 41

Cutting Squares from Strips - Page 42

Double Check Your Cuts - Page 43

Helpful Cutting Habits - Page 43

Cutting Scraps Accurately - Page 44

Materials Needed for Fabric Cutting

Self-healing cutting mat in an ugly color

A self-healing cutting mat is a special mat that can be sliced with a rotary cutter or blade and absorb the cut.

Either pick an ugly color or a color you'll never use in fabric because you need a sharp contrast between the color of the mat and the color of the fabric. An 18 x 24 inch mat is a great size and will accommodate most projects.

If you can find one, look for a cutting mat with no printed lines on the surface. The lines on a cutting mat might appear accurately printed, but in truth they're rarely lines you can trust for fabric cutting.

Don't worry if you can't find a mat without printed lines. We're going to learn how to cut without using these lines so it honestly doesn't matter if it's marked or not.

Just remember if you've gotten into the habit of using printed lines to now ignore them completely. From here on out, the only lines you'll be using for measuring and cutting are the lines on your cutting rulers.

Cutting rulers

Clear rulers are the key to cutting fabric accurately. You'll want to **pick one brand of rulers** and stick with just that one brand. The reason for this is simple: all rulers are created and printed in their own unique way.

Some rulers have fat lines where the fabric needs to line up with the middle of the line, while others have thinner lines that need to be included in the measurement as you cut the fabric.

Switching from one type of ruler to another can be both confusing and a recipe for disastrous cutting mistakes! Make sure when you're selecting your rulers that you can see the lines very clearly. **Visibility is key** and if you can't see the lines, the ruler is going to be useless.

The most helpful sizes to own are a 12 ½-inch square ruler and a 6 x 24 inch rectangle ruler. You can cut the pieces for almost any quilt using just these two rulers!

> **Leah's Note:** *When I started quilting in 2009 I purchased a set of Optima rulers, which have since been discontinued.*
>
> *After trying many different brands I've found the Olfa frosted rulers to have thin lines and excellent visibility.*
>
> *Best of all, the frosted back grips fabric so you don't have to add InvisiGrip to the back.*

Gripping material

Cutting rulers are typically made of thick acrylic plastic, which is terrific to see through and cut against, but can be slippery when placed on top of fabric.

To make the ruler less likely to slip, you'll need to cover the back side with a grippy material that will cling to the fabric and help the ruler stay in place as you cut.

InvisiGrip is an invisible gripping material you can cut to size and smooth over the back of your rulers. It's completely invisible and once stuck to the back, it doesn't peel off or interfere with measuring or cutting in any way.

Another alternative is sandpaper dots, but these little grippy stickers are not clear, so they can impede your vision as you line up fabric with your measurements. They also only cover small spaces on the ruler, making it less stable when cutting.

Some new rulers are manufactured with a gripping material on the back side. This is yet another feature to consider when investing in your rulers.

Rotary cutter

This is the cutting tool that looks a bit like a pizza cutter and is used to slice your fabric into precise pieces. When shopping for a cutter don't go super cheap, but don't go crazy expensive either.

Fiskars produces a very nice line of cutters that are comfortable, have good safety features, and use relatively inexpensive replacement blades.

Always check the prices of the blades before buying your cutter. Some cutters, like Fiskars, have a standard attachment so that any brand of blade will fit. Other cutters require you to purchase brand-named blades, which can get expensive.

Cutter size – An average rotary cutter blade will last through 2-3 quilt projects. 45 mm cutters are the most common and popular size.

The larger the blade, the fewer times it has to revolve to cut a particular length of fabric, so the less wear and tear on the blade. Cutting with a larger blade is also easier, with more control over the blade staying right against the side of the rotary ruler.

> **Leah's Note:** *I use only 60 mm rotary cutter blades because they're bigger and easier to handle, and wear out far less often than the smaller blades. Bigger is better when it comes to blades!*

Comfortable working surface

You don't want to try to cut fabric in a dark room on the floor. Find a room in your home with great light and a table at a comfortable height.

Having a permanent setup for your cutting materials is convenient and practical considering that you will probably spend just as much time cutting your fabric as you spend piecing it.

DIRECTIONS FOR FABRIC CUTTING

It's time to start cutting! We've squared our fabric to the grain lines using the fabric dance and it's folded on our cutting table, ready to be cut into the pieces for a quilt.

The next step will be to use the fold line we've just created to square off one edge of the fabric. This first cut edge should form a perfect 90-degree angle to the fold.

Remember: When lining up your fabric to trim or cut, it's important to line up the ruler, measure and cut with the ruler on the fabric, not the lines on the cutting mat, which are rarely accurate.

First square up cut

Lay your ruler over your fabric, lining up a horizontal line on the ruler with the fold line in the fabric. We line up the ruler this way so the bulk of the ruler is on the fabric and lined up with the fold.

Left-handed first cut

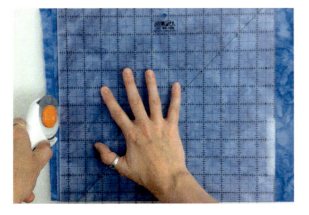

Right-handed first cut

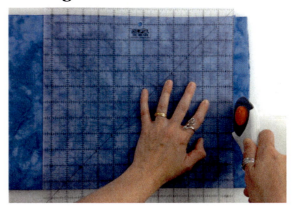

Press the ruler firmly in place over the fabric and set the rotary blade against the edge of the ruler. Cut carefully away from your body with a smooth motion, keeping the blade tight against the edge of the ruler. If you're right-handed, you'll hold the ruler with your left hand and the cutter with your right. Left-handers will hold the cutter in their left hand and the ruler with their right.

For this first cut, you will typically slice off ½ inch of fabric to square the edge. Depending on how out of square the fabric was, you may need to slice off more fabric to square the edge perfectly.

After making this first cut, the bottom fold should form a perfect 90 degree angle to the cut edge. If you look closely, the threads in the fabric should run perfectly parallel and perpendicular to this cut edge.

Leah's Note - *If you had to make multiple passes to cut your fabric, change your blade. It's too dull to cut properly and will cause more problems for your fabric and project if you continue to use it.*

Fabric flip

After making the first square-up cut, carefully flip your fabric over so the cut edge is on the opposite side. This way you can measure your strips accurately and make every cut with your dominant hand, which will give you the most control over your rotary cutter.

CUTTING STRIPS PERFECTLY

Most fabric is first cut into strips and then cut down into squares or rectangles as needed for your quilt pattern.

Let's now line up our ruler on the fabric and cut a 2 ½-inch strip. First line up a horizontal line on the ruler with the fold line of the fabric. Don't use the bottom edge of your ruler as it's tricky to see the edge and line up with the fold properly.

Next line up the 2 ½-inch mark on the ruler with the cut edge of the fabric. Both the fold and cut edge should line up perfectly on these straight lines of the ruler. With the ruler in place, cutting this strip will look like this:

Left-handed strip cut

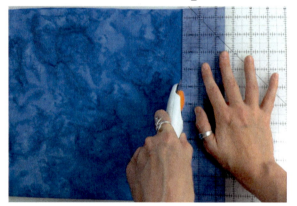

Right-handed strip cut

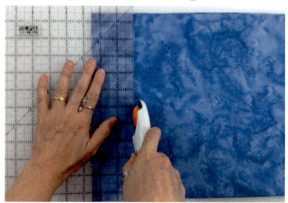

Using a firm pressure on your ruler, make the cut with your rotary cutter moving away from you. Again, if you have to make multiple passes to cut the fabric with your rotary cutter, you need to change the blade or apply more pressure on the cutter as you cut.

Width-of-fabric strips – When you cut strips this way, they are often described in patterns as "Width of Fabric" which means a strip that's cut from selvage to selvage across the width of the fabric yardage. Width-of-fabric strips are typically 40 to 44 inches long.

What if the lines don't line up perfectly?

*If you can't align your ruler with both the cut fabric edge and fold line at once, this means the fabric is **not perfectly square.***

Somewhere along the line maybe the ruler slipped with the first cut, or the fabric went wonky when you flipped it – regardless, you'll need to start over again. Pick up the fabric and shake it out. Square the grain line again by doing the fabric dance and repeat all the steps to get back to this point.

Yes, this might feel a bit annoying at first, but once you get into the habit of squaring your fabric, it will be a quick reset - dance, fold, trim the edge, and back to cutting.

Measuring Correctly

As you are measuring this 2 ½-inch strip, or any piece of fabric, remember to INCLUDE the line you are cutting to. Yes, that little black line needs to be included in the cut strip.

Why? The rulers illustrated here use thin black lines to indicate the measurements. These lines are intended to be included in the measurement for the square to measure exactly 2 ½ inches.

Without the line included, you are cutting the shape **two to three threads too small.** As picky as it may seem, cutting pieces that are one or two threads off can make a very big difference on your quilt.

Lost Thread Calculation

Let's assume that two threads of material measures around 1/32 of an inch. You have a Four Patch block that's made up of 16, 2 ½-inch squares, so it should piece to 8 ½ inches square.

But if you lose two threads on EACH SIDE for each piece, by the time you get done with your block, you have lost ¼ inch from the length and width of this block.

Instead of measuring 8 ½ inches, this incorrectly cut block will measure 8 ¼ inches, a full ¼ inch off.

Consistency is key

If you were consistently off with every single one of your pieces then this issue wouldn't actually be a very big problem.

Your quilt would finish smaller, but because all the pieces were consistently cut small, you probably wouldn't have too much trouble matching up your seams.

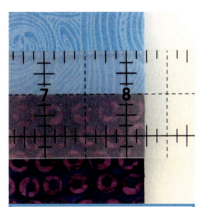

Lost threads in cutting caused this block to finish ¼ inch too small!

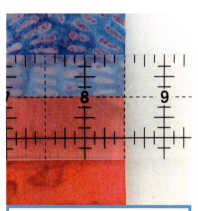

Cut correctly this block measures the correct size: 8 ½ inches square

This assumes you cut ALL pieces excluding the line and shorting the pieces by EXACTLY the same amount.

The trouble is most quilters are not consistent with cutting. If you cut half of your pieces including the line and half of the pieces excluding the line, then you will be in for a world of hurt when it comes to matching up these blocks.

This is why many quilters struggle to match seams when piecing: **Incorrect and inconsistent cutting.**

To cut correctly ALWAYS make sure the line on the ruler is included in the shape you are cutting.

ONE TO RULE THEM ALL

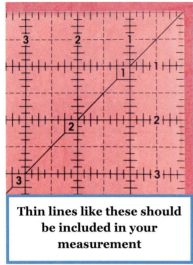

Thin lines like these should be included in your measurement

Rulers with thicker lines align the fabric to the middle of the line

Because it's so important to include the lines of the ruler in your measurement, it's a good idea to stick with one brand of rulers for all fabric cutting.

Different rulers have different line widths. For some, the inch marks will be wider than the other marks, while on other brands all marks are the same size. It can be very confusing to switch from one brand to another with different markings and line widths. Switching continually is also a good way to make big cutting mistakes.

It's also important to use the same brand of ruler because each brand produces rulers to different specifications. This may sound weird. ***Isn't one inch is always one inch?***

It is, but what if you were using a ruler brand that had extremely wide lines? These lines were designed for you to measure to the MIDDLE of the line. But you can't see your fabric under the line so you have no idea where it's lining up.

Be very careful when picking your ruler brand. If you've already purchased several rulers from many different companies, sort them and figure out which brand is your favorite. Sell or give away the rulers that don't match your chosen brand.

This might sound wasteful, but remember you only need a **12 ½-inch square ruler and a 6 x 24 inch rectangle to cut the pieces of almost any quilt project.**

Manufacturers want us all to collect fifty rulers of all shapes and sizes because it makes them more money. It's completely unnecessary to have this much junk cluttering up our sewing spaces when we really can only ever use one ruler at a time!

If you're new to quilting, go to a store with several brands on display and play with them against both light and dark fabrics. Can you see the lines clearly? Is there a sharp contrast between the lines and the fabric?

If you can't see it, you can't cut it accurately. You have to be able to see exactly where the edges of the piece line up on the ruler, and you must be able to include the full amount of the line needed to have a piece cut at the full, proper size.

> **Leah's Note:** *Being able to SEE the fabric edge under the ruler is the most important thing to look for in a ruler.*
>
> *If you can't see, you can't cut accurately!*

Yes, it takes time to cut each piece, making sure to square your fabric and include the line with each cut. But it's also a foolproof method for knowing that every piece you cut is perfect and ready to be pieced properly.

So get into the habit today of including the cutting line with every slice you make. **Starting today, every piece you cut will be exactly the right size.**

CUTTING STRAIGHT STRIPS

Let's take a closer look at the 2 ½-inch strip you've just cut. After cutting your strip, unfold it and look at all of the fold lines. A full length 44-inch strip will have three fold lines.

Each fold line represents a spot for us to check our work so far. If the fold was square to the grain line of the fabric, and cut straight, the fabric should also form a perfectly straight strip even through the fold.

Below is a photo of two cut strips. The first strip was cut straight and on-grain. When unfolded, the strip runs straight along the lines on the cutting mat.

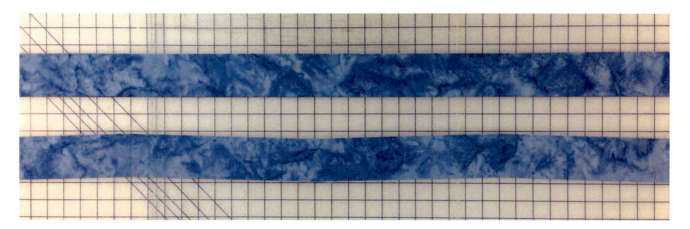

The second strip in the photo was cut off-grain. Notice how it doesn't run straight with the lines on the mat, but instead forms almost a wave or zigzag. This is caused by cutting off-grain across the folds of the fabric.

Where did the problem happen?

Two easy cutting mistakes cause this to happen:

1) The fabric wasn't squared properly before it was cut.

   Solution - Do the fabric dance and square properly before cutting.

2) The fabric was square, but the ruler slipped during the first square-up cut.

   Solution - If you can't line up both the fold and cut edge of your fabric with straight lines on your ruler, the fabric is no longer square. Do the fabric dance and repeat the first square-up cut.

Also be very attentive to your ruler - if it slips even slightly, stop and trim the edge square before proceeding with any more cuts. Otherwise every cut you make will be incorrect.

Yes, you may lose ½ inch of fabric every time you cut the edge square. This is not wasteful because cutting fabric perfectly will make your piecing experience so much easier and faster in the long run.

Cutting Squares from Strips

So far we've focused on cutting 2 ½-inch strips. Now let's cut one strip down into 2 ½-inch squares.

Step 1 - Unfold and check the strip - It's a good habit to completely unfold a strip and check that the fabric is cut straight through the fold lines. The top and bottom edges of this strip should be straight and square to the grain line of the fabric, so they will be the lines we trust on the fabric to line up with our ruler.

Step 2 - First square-up cut - Next, let's square off the end so we have three straight sides to work with. This will also remove the selvage - the thicker, printed edge of the fabric, which we don't want to include in our piece.

Line up two straight, horizontal lines on the ruler with the top and bottom edges of the cut strip. Trim off the selvage edge.

Left-handed first cut   **Right-handed first cut**

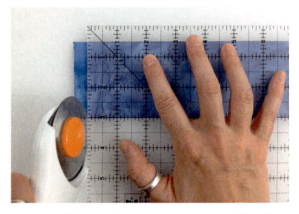 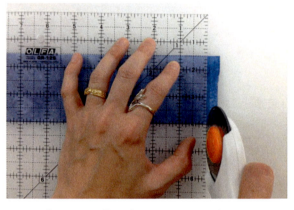

Step 3 - Flip and cut squares - Flip the strip over so the cut edge is now opposite your dominant hand. Line up the top and bottom edges of the strip with horizontal lines on your ruler, and the 2 ½-inch mark with the cut end of the strip. Double check to include the 2 ½-inch mark in your measurement. With firm pressure on your ruler, make the cut away from you:

Always remember the golden rule: Measure Twice, Cut Once!

Left-handed cutting 2 ½-inch square   **Right-handed cutting 2 ½-inch square**

 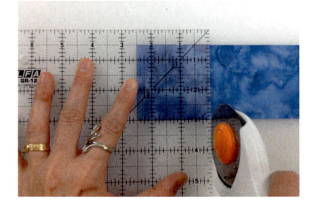

DOUBLE CHECK YOUR CUTS

After cutting your first 2 ½-inch square, check the accuracy of your piece by laying your ruler on top.

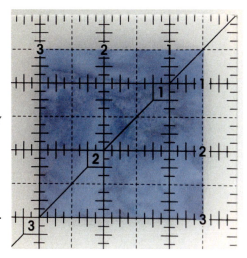

The square should fill up the entire 2 ½-inch space, including the lines on the ruler.

The square on the right is cut perfectly - the shape perfectly measures 2 ½ inches and the visible grain lines of the fabric are parallel with the cut edges of the square.

What if the square is a bit big?

If the shape you have cut is bigger than the 2 ½-inch measurement, even by two threads extending beyond the ruler line, you should take the time to correct it.

Simply trim the square down to the correct size by lining up one corner with the 2 ½-inch marks on the ruler and any extra fabric that extends beyond the side and top of the ruler.

What if the square is a bit small?

There's a reason the golden rule is Measure Twice, Cut Once! If you cut your shape too small, yes, even by two or three threads, **you will need to cut the piece again.**

The reason is simple: If the shape is cut too small, it will not fit with shapes that were cut the correct size.

We learned about this issue on page 39 - incorrect and inconsistent cutting is the initial culprit behind mismatching seams. The pieces must be cut the same size in order to contain the same amount of seam allowance.

Remember in Chapter 1 - quilting is a simple process of adding seam allowance, then taking it away. If a piece is not cut correctly, the simple math of quilting simply won't work.

Yes, in the beginning it may seem tedious to be constantly checking and double checking your work this way. Ultimately this process will get faster as you bring these extra steps into your cutting routine and build habits for checking your work.

HELPFUL CUTTING HABITS:

- As you cut multiple strips, double check the folds in every fifth strip. If the strip shows any sign of the "V" shape through the fold, shake out the fabric and square the edge again.
- When cutting multiple pieces from strips, flip the strip over and square up the edge every fifth cut.
- Double check the size of your pieces by placing a ruler on top and checking the shape is square, the grain lines run parallel with the cut edges, and that it's cut exactly the correct size.
- The most important tip of all: **Take your time cutting fabric!**

Cutting Scraps Accurately

Many quilters like to work with scraps. We are all very frugal by nature and the idea of throwing away good fabric just because it's oddly shaped is just unthinkable to most quilters.

If you're a scrap fan, you already understand that there will be situations where you can't cut your pieces from strips or even properly square your fabric because it's in such a weird piece. It's times like these that you have to rely on your eyesight, high-powered lighting, and grain line. Let's cut a few 2 ½-inch squares together from scraps:

Step 1 - Starch and press - Starching and pressing will stabilize your fabric and make it easier to cut accurately. Pull out the scraps you plan to use and spray starch over the right side. Flip the scrap over and press from the wrong side to bond the starch to the fabric.

Step 2 - Find the grain - Take your scrap and lay it on your cutting mat. Turn on a very bright, high powered lamp and look at the lines of threads. It might even help to pull a few threads loose on one edge so you can clearly see the direction the threads are running.

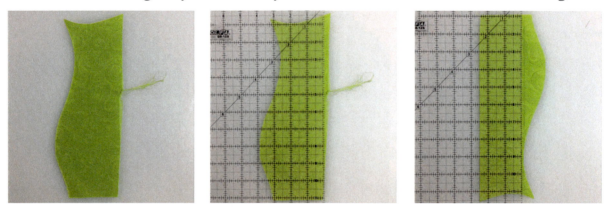

Step 3 - First cut - Line up your ruler parallel with the thread lines on the scrap. Yes, they are hard to see. That's why you need the high-powered lighting! Take your time lining up for this first cut as all other cuts will be based on it.

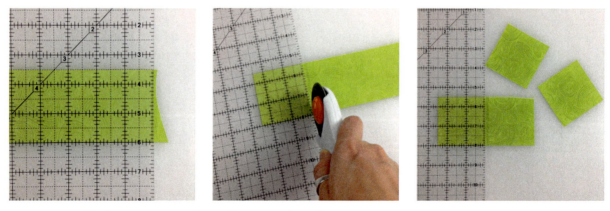

Step 4 - Parallel cut - Now align the straight edge you just cut with the 2 ½-inch mark on your ruler. Holding the ruler firmly in place, make this second cut parallel to the first.

Step 5 - Cut squares from the strip - Now you can treat the scrap just like a strip of fabric. Square off the end and cut as many squares as possible from the scrap. Take your time finding and cutting with the grain line of each fabric scrap so every piece is cut on-grain and exactly the correct shape and size.

~ Chapter 6 ~
Basic Machine Piecing

So far we've learned how to properly prepare our fabric and cut it into exact pieces that are ready to be pieced together into blocks. Piecing is actually very, very simple. Using either a sewing machine or hand stitches, blocks are sewn together using a ¼-inch seam allowance. This seam allowance connects the pieces together with the least amount of waste.

*There is one fundamental rule to all piecing – **whatever you add in seam allowance, you take away with the seam, leaving the exact shape needed on the surface of your quilt.***

Chapter 6 Sections:

Machine Piecing Tools and Equipment - Page 46

How to Rip Stitches Out - Page 51

How to Piece by Machine - Page 52

Anatomy of a Seam - Page 53

Checking Seams - Page 54

Scant Quarter Confusion - Page 54

Don't I Need to Backstitch? - Page 55

Seam Allowances - Open or Over? - Page 55

Seam Allowance Math - Page 56

Accuracy and Precision - Page 57

Matching Seams Perfectly - Page 58

Troubleshooting Mismatched Seams - Page 60

Machine Piecing Tools and Equipment

Sewing machine

Sewing machines are available in an amazing range of prices and features. New machines can range from $100 to several thousand, and yes, it is generally true that you get what you pay for in a sewing machine. Unfortunately, not all sewing machines are truly worth their salt and it's extremely important to use a machine that works properly.

Numerous novice quilters have been turned off from this hobby, not due to lack of skill, but because they spend all their time fighting with their machine. Nothing can be more frustrating than attempting to piece a beautiful quilt, only to see your fabric being eaten by the machine.

Finding a good sewing machine for piecing really doesn't have to drive you into deep debt, but one feature you need to be able to control on your machine is the stitch length.

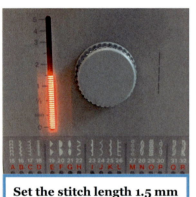

Set the stitch length 1.5 mm

In order to sew accurate and precise seams it's also important to use a tighter stitch length than you may be used to. **Set your stitch length to 1.5 mm** and see how tight and secure this seam line is in comparison to the factory setting on your machine.

This tighter stitch length accomplishes many things: it locks the cotton fabrics together in a seam that is so secure we can press the seam allowances open, which results in far more accurately pieced blocks. The tighter stitch length also makes the thread take up less space in the seam allowance.

Compare the two lines of stitching in the photo on the left. The top row is stitched with the machine default setting of 2.0 mm, and the bottom row was set to 1.5 mm.

Leah's Note - *While it's beyond the scope of this book to dig into the issue of the best machine for piecing, I will share my favorite machine for quilt piecing – Bernina.*

I have owned multiple Bernina sewing machines and found every one to be a solid piecing machine with beautiful stitch quality and long lasting durability.

Currently I use an **older Bernina 1230** *shown in the left photo, which is still an amazing machine for piecing and applique.*

Patchwork or ¼-inch feet

A well-designed piecing foot is absolutely essential for piecing perfect seams. The alternative is using a regular foot and moving your needle over to the left or right to create a ¼-inch seam allowance.

However, a piecing foot is much more accurate because the edge measures exactly ¼-inch from the center needle position and doesn't require the needle to move.

The trick to remember with a piecing foot is that the edge of the foot exactly measures ¼ inch. This means that no fabric should extend past the side of the foot, not even a single thread.

Watch out for feet that include fabric guides along either side. The idea behind a guide is simple - line up the edge of your fabric with the guide and speed stitch every seam.

Unfortunately this supposed time saver is actually an impediment to perfect piecing. Most guides are made from cheap, flimsy metal that easily bends if you apply the slightest pressure against it.

If you're a heavy-handed piecer and feed the fabric against the guide with too much pressure, you could easily be stitching with a seam allowance bigger than ¼ inch.

With the guide in place, you also can't see where the fabric is lining up under the foot.

If you can't see the edge of the foot or the edge of the fabric, you can't piece accurately because you have no idea if the fabric is lining up exactly with the edge of the foot. You could easily stitch a smaller or wider seam without knowing it because the metal guide is blocking your vision.

Not even a single thread should show past the edge of your patchwork foot

Avoid feet with guides as they can block your view of the fabric edge

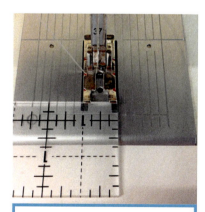

The Bernina patchwork foot measures ¼" from either side of the needle

Leah's Note - *One of the main reasons I love Bernina sewing machines for piecing is the Bernina patchwork foot, which is a wonderfully designed foot that accurately measures ¼ inch from either side of the center.*

This allows you to line up the edge of your fabric piece with the edge of your foot and reliably stitch a perfect ¼-inch seam every time.

If you don't have a Bernina machine, or can't find this patchwork foot, look for a foot that measures ¼ inch to either side of the needle.

Many feet only measure the ¼-inch seam allowance to the right side, which is annoying for certain binding techniques that require using the opposite edge of the foot.

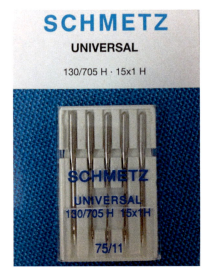

Needles

When was the last time you changed the needle in your machine? If you can't remember, it's definitely time to change the needle. **One of the most important quilting habits is to change sewing needles often.**

After you've emptied your bobbin twice, follow these steps: change the needle, brush out the base of the machine, and apply a drop of oil where needed. Your machine and next project will thank you!

As for the TYPE of needle you use - there are a lot of choices: Universal, Top Stitch, Microtex, Sharp, etc., and each type has specific characteristics like a blunted or sharp point which can change the way it pierces the fabric and ultimately affect your results.

Which needle is the best for quilt piecing? It really depends on your machine and the thread you're using. It's a good idea to play with different types of needles and sizes to find what works best.

A good size to start with is an 80/12, but if you're piecing very small blocks with very fine thread, a 75/11 or 70/10 might be a good size to try. When shopping for needles, you will find that the larger the number on the package, the larger the needle.

> **Leah's Note -** *There are now so many brands and so many types of needles that the choices can be quite overwhelming. I find the most practical way to approach picking needles is to start with what you have on hand. If your thread is constantly breaking or knotting up, that's a sign you need to try a different needle to see if it will work better.*
>
> *My personal favorite needles are Schmetz Universal size 80/12 needles because they work great in all my machines for both piecing and quilting.*
>
> *Even more important than the size or type is the habit of changing needles often. I once spoke to a machine repairman who said 99% of all machine issues are fixed by simply changing the needle in the machine!*

Fabric marking pencil

For piecing, you will need a very fine marking tool that produces marks you can see clearly, but also erase when you no longer need them. Whatever marking pencil you decide to use, make sure to first test it on a scrap of fabric from your project. The worst feeling in the world is realizing you've just marked and pieced 20 flying geese blocks with a purple pen, only to realize that that pen was permanent!

> **Leah's Note -** *I use the* **Fons & Porter Ceramic Pencil** *for piecing and quilting. The marks it creates are clearly visible and bold, but can be easily erased with the eraser on the pencil or brushed off with a damp paper towel.*

Thread

For piecing, 100% cotton thread is a good choice for piecing cotton fabrics together. The main reason is the fibers in the cotton thread will "lock" with the fibers in the cotton fabric, creating a seam that will be very difficult to pick out or unravel.

The most important thing when it comes to thread is making sure that it doesn't take up too much space in your seam allowance. Thicker, heavy weight threads will take up more space and can throw your seam allowance off, sometimes by more than 1/16th inch.

For thread sizes, the bigger the number, the thinner the thread will be. A good weight to look for in thread is 40 or 50 weight, which is thin enough not to take up too much space in the seam.

Another feature to pay close attention to is the amount of lint in your spool of thread. Some cotton threads are so filled with lint and dust, they could easily clog up the moving parts around your bobbin case and feed dogs and lock up your machine.

Unfortunately, it's hard to know which threads will be thick or linty in the store. This is yet another material you will need to test in order to know what works in your machine and gives you the results you like.

If you notice your machine running loud or making noticeable clicking noises, that's a sure sign your machine needs a good clean out. Follow the instructions in your machine manual to remove the covers around your bobbin case so you can brush out the lint and apply oil where needed.

Old thread alert - Cotton thread actually has a shelf life. Over time and exposure to damp air and light, cotton thread can weaken, which will result in frequent thread breaks and bird's nests on your machine.

You might have already experienced this as a spool of new but "bad" thread that continually broke, no matter how you threaded your machine or set your tension.

Exposure to light and moisture will quickly deteriorate thread, so it's a good idea to keep your cotton thread protected, either in a drawer or in a plastic case.

Most cotton thread will last reliably for one year, but after that time, it's probably a good idea to replace it. It's far easier to buy a new spool than try to piece with thread that makes your machine continually gag.

Watch out for threads that produce lots of lint, which could clog the feed dogs of your machine

Leah's Note - *For piecing and general sewing I use **Aurifil 50 wt. cotton**, which is a super thin, practically lint-free thread that takes up minimal space inside the seam allowance.*

Patchwork pins

When piecing blocks and quilts, accurate pinning is important to match seams perfectly. You will place pins in the seam allowance, about 1/8 inch from the seam line. This means your pins will need to slide through four layers of fabric smoothly and hold securely.

Thicker pins will be impossible to insert through so many layers of fabric. If you find yourself struggling to insert a pin, this is a sure sign it's too thick for the job.

Be on the lookout for fine patchwork pins with a 0.5 mm shaft. These thinner pins will slide into multiple fabrics easily, and are thin enough you can stitch over them very carefully when piecing tricky seams.

Also look for pins with glass heads which are easier to grip than pins with no heads. Glass head pins can also be ironed over unlike plastic pins.

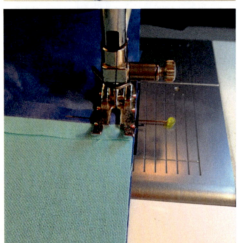

> **Leah's Note** - *Yes, I am very guilty of stitching over my pins when piecing tricky seams. I've found that so long as I stitch very slowly, and I work with very fine pins, I never hit the pin directly with my needle. This helps maintain control over tricky seams and guarantees a perfect match every time.*

Machine and desk lights

Good lighting is crucial for machine piecing. For some reason most machines have lights installed on the left side of the needle, which is the opposite side we usually use for piecing.

You need a bright light on the right side of your needle to illuminate the right edge of your patchwork foot. This is the edge you will align with your fabrics to piece almost every seam you stitch for your quilts.

It's worth the investment to buy specific sewing machine lights like the **Ecolux sewing machine lights**. These LED lights install on the underside of your machine arm to provide brighter light around your needle area.

It's also important to have bright desk lamps close by to illuminate the entire sewing table. When piecing a large quilt, you may have the quilt in your lap aligning seams and pinning. Floor or desk lamps directed from over your shoulder will greatly improve your ability to see for these tasks.

> **Leah's Note** - *I began using high powered LED machine lights in 2014 and immediately noticed a difference in my piecing and quilting ability.*
>
> *If you can't see what you are doing, you can't piece perfectly!*

Seam ripper

Unfortunately, ripping out seams is an occupational hazard for anyone wanting to learn how to piece perfectly. You might as well work with a comfortable seam ripper that fits nicely in your hand.

Look for a seam ripper like the **Clover ripper** on the right which has a thin, sharp blade. You will need a very tiny blade in order to slide into small stitches easily.

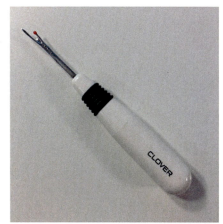

How to Rip Stitches Out

If you wish to piece absolutely perfect blocks and quilts, you will need to accept that ripping stitches is going to be part of this process. This is so important, we're going to learn how to rip stitches out before we even learn how to piece our first seam.

Use this method to rip out stitches most efficiently so you can quickly get back to piecing.

1. Pick one side of the seam and begin ripping by inserting the blade of the seam ripper into the stitch and pressing away from you gently to rip the thread.

2. Rip every 4th stitch along the length of the stitching line.

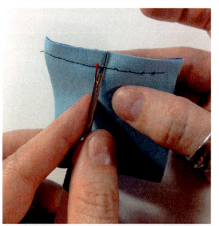

3. Flip the piece over and locate the thread on the opposite side of the seam you just ripped. Give it a tug and all the stitches will pull out quickly.

4. Pull out all the tiny stray threads to clean up the fabrics before piecing the seam again.

5. Take your time to figure out what went wrong so you don't repeat the same mistake again.

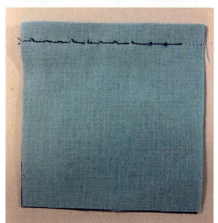

Yes, continually ripping is time consuming, so as you make mistakes, try to find the culprit that threw off your piecing. Was your seam allowance a little big or a little small? Could you have pinned the pieces better to match the seam lines?

One thing you should NOT do while ripping is beat yourself up for making mistakes. Mistakes are part of the learning process so forgive yourself for making the error and rip out the stitches quickly so you can get back to piecing your project.

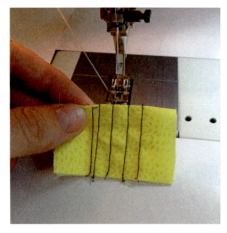

How to Piece by Machine

The steps to machine piecing are the same, no matter if you're piecing 2 ½-inch squares or 44-inch long strips. Let's learn how to piece accurately and precisely through all the parts of the seam.

Start with a scrap charger - You need to start with a perfect ¼" seam allowance, but sometimes your fabric won't feed nicely or the bobbin thread will gag on you just as you're getting started. There's a very simple solution to this called a scrap charger.

A scrap charger is a 2 ½-inches scrap of fabric that's been folded in half. Stitch through this doubled scrap, and stop with your needle in the down position as you stitch off the edge.

Remember to drop your stitch length to 1.5 mm so the stitches are tiny and super secure!

This little scrap of fabric helps to get your presser foot up a little higher so your fabrics will feed nice and evenly underneath it. It also eliminates the annoying gagging and bobbin thread buildup that sometimes happens when you're just getting started. All of that mess gets sorted out on the charger, not on the pieces of your block.

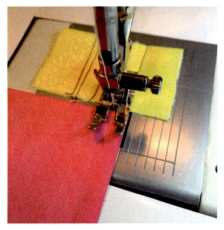

First crucial stitches - Pick up two 2 ½-inch squares of fabric and hold them right sides together. Take your time to align all four sides together. You want to make sure that the two pieces are in perfect alignment so they will piece properly together.

Gently lift the presser foot lightly with a knee lifter, or if you don't have one, very slightly with your hand. Slip your pieces under the presser foot until they're right next to the needle. The next stitch you take will start stitching the pieces together.

As you are aligning the pieces next to the needle, also align the right edge along the right edge of the presser foot. If you're using a ¼-inch piecing foot, there should be no fabric or thread exposed on the right hand side of the foot.

Take a few careful stitches, holding the two fabrics together with gentle pressure from your fingertips. Make sure the edge of the fabrics stay aligned perfectly with the right edge of the foot. The fabric edge should not extend beyond this edge, not even by a single thread! If the fabric extends beyond the edge of the foot, you are piecing with too big a seam allowance.

Also make sure the edge of the fabric doesn't drift inward, under the foot where you can't see the edge clearly. Lift the foot often to double check the edge of the fabrics stay perfectly aligned with the edge of the presser foot. If you stitch with the fabrics drifting under the foot, you are piecing with too small a seam allowance.

Stay on track - The middle section of the seam is the easiest part because you only need to focus on keeping the fabric aligned with the edge of the presser foot.

However this is the section of any seam where you need to be especially vigilant. It's easy to start daydreaming and if your mind wanders off, so does your proper seam allowance.

It's important to pay attention during the middle of any seam because this is where we have the best opportunity to practice stitching a straight line. Slow down, resist slamming the pedal to the metal, and be vigilant in keeping the fabrics aligned with the edge of the presser foot.

Finish the seam accurately - The end of the seam is so rarely even noticed, who knows if it's accurate or not? By the time you reach the last inch of the seam, you're probably already reaching for your next piece, glass of water, or chocolate bar, and not paying the slightest attention to the piece you're finishing.

Resist the need for speed! Again, maintain your concentration and keep your stitches precisely on the ¼-inch seam allowance. Don't start fiddling around for your next piece!

Finishing up - Take about three stitches off your piece and then stop with the needle down. Run another scrap charger under your presser foot, ending with the needle in the down position. Now your sewing machine is ready for the next seam.

Clip your fabric piece from the scrap charger and open the seam gently with your fingertips. Opening the seam with your fingertips will be much gentler than forcing the seam allowances open with the tip of your iron.

Once the seam allowance is finger pressed, set the piece on your pressing board and gently press the seam allowances open with a hot, dry iron.

ANATOMY OF A SEAM

Every seam has the following features:

A - Edge where the fabrics are aligned with the edge of your patchwork foot

B - Line of stitching exactly 1/4 inch away from the edge

C - Seam allowance now clearly visible between the stitching line and fabric edge

D - Seam line on the right side which you'll want to match with the seam line on other pieces. This is also called the "ditch" between the pieces.

The key to piecing every seam perfectly lies in keeping the edge of the fabrics aligned with the edge of the presser foot

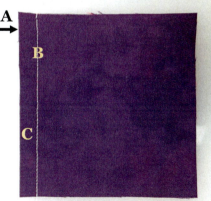

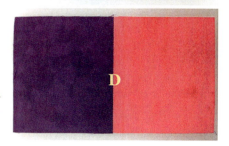

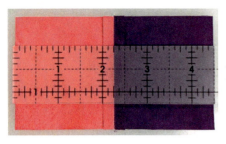

CHECKING SEAMS

After finishing a seam, lay the pieces out on the table where you can see the stitches you've just sewn. Take a ruler and put a line over your stitches. You're checking now to see if your stitches have been sewn straight, accurately, and with precision.

If you can't line up your ruler with the line of stitching, that means your stitching wasn't sewn straight. Rip out the seam and sew it again.

If you line up your ruler, but the seam allowance goes past the ¼-inch mark then you've stitched the seam too big. Rip out the seam and sew it again. If you line up your ruler with the stitching and the seam allowance doesn't reach the ¼-inch line, then you sewed a seam that was too small. Rip out the seam and stitch it again.

Getting the drift yet? Your seam ripper is your new best friend! Precise and accurate piecing may require much more work than you're used to. You may find yourself ripping out seams constantly until it becomes habit to stitch each seam perfectly, every time.

> *Leah's Note* - I don't like to use the term scant quarter because it's confusing.
>
> No matter if you piece with a ¼ inch seam allowance with thin thread or scant quarter with thicker thread, the ultimate measurement of the block should finish the same.

SCANT QUARTER CONFUSION

A lot of confusion is created in quilting by the notion of a scant quarter, which is a measurement describing ¼ inch minus one thread width. In other words - a tiny bit less than ¼ inch.

Scant quarter seam allowances came about because many quilters stitched a seam with thicker thread, then measured the resulting piece and found it was a little off. The thread was taking up space in the seam allowance and widening the seam by one to two threads worth of space.

So the solution was to still cut pieces with the same ¼-inch seam allowance, but piece with a scant quarter --slightly smaller than ¼ inch --so the extra space taken up by the thread could be accounted for and the piece or block would still measure the correct size.

How do you know if you're piecing with a scant quarter or not? Really this depends entirely on the foot you are using for piecing. Most patchwork feet measure exactly ¼ inch from the center needle position to the right side, but some actually measure a scant quarter instead.

Stitch two squares together and measure the seam allowance. Is the thread line exactly ¼ inch away from the edge of the pieces, or slightly LESS than ¼ inch?

If it's exactly ¼ inch away, just make sure to piece with thin, 50 weight cotton thread and to lower your stitch length to 1.5 mm. This will ensure the thread takes up minimal space in the seam and you still end up with blocks pieced the correct size.

If you have a scant quarter foot, you won't need to worry so much about the thickness of your piecing thread because it's accounted in that slightly smaller stitched seam allowance. Ultimately, no matter if you are piecing with a ¼ inch or scant quarter, the key is consistency. Use the same seam allowance on every single seam and you should have no trouble piecing any block or quilt perfectly.

Don't I Need to Backstitch?

No, for most machine piecing, you don't need to backstitch at the beginning and end of the seams.

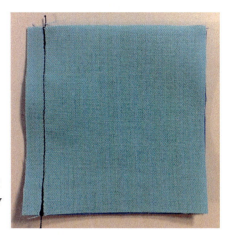

Backstitching will actually create a build-up of thread at the beginning and end of the seam, which could reduce the size of the seam allowance, and make it harder to match your seams.

If you're using thin cotton thread and cotton fabric and a short 1.5 mm stitch length, your stitches not only never unravel, they will be nearly impossible to rip out!

Seam Allowances - Open or Over?

Many quilters prefer to press both seam allowances over to one side rather than open.

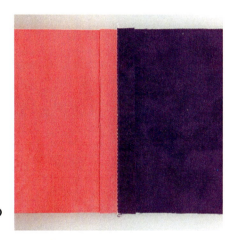

Yes, pressing to one side is faster because you don't have to stop and finger press the seam. Using your iron, you can force both seams to one side with a quick press.

Many quilters also like this method because the noticeable hump created by the seam allowances can be used to "lock" pieces together as you're matching up seams.

However, by pressing to one side, you're actually shrinking your block in an unpredictable way. The two fabrics pressed to one side rarely open fully, so several threads worth of fabric are eaten up by the fold to one side.

> *Pressing seam allowances to one side reduces the size of the piece, which will add up quickly in piece after piece, block after block, and result in an imperfectly pieced quilt.*

And what if you spend more time pressing the seam allowance in some blocks and less time pressing others? Yep, you're back to the situation of rampant inconsistency – every block will measure a little different and no seams will match up perfectly.

Speaking of matching, the feeling of "locking" pieces together when the seam allowances are pressed to opposite sides is not a predictable technique you can depend on. Because the bulky seam allowances are throwing off the size of the cut shape, our simple math equation is not going to work and our blocks will not finish the proper size.

Worse than the inaccuracy, the noticeable hump creates an even more noticeable lump in the finished quilt that can be very difficult to quilt over. While this book is focused solely on piecing, this is one area where the construction of the quilt and the choices you make now will affect how easy it will be to finish your quilt later.

Yes, as you first start to match seams with the seam allowances pressed open, you will have to expend more effort to match the seam lines perfectly. A little extra effort is well worth the ultimate goal of perfectly pieced blocks and quilts!

Seam Allowance Math

A 2 ½ inch square is cut, but ¼ inch all around the edge is seam allowance

Now that we've pieced several 2 ½-inch squares together, let's dig more into the math behind the piecing. It's important to understand that once we piece these squares into a quilt they will finish at 2 inches – ½ inch smaller than the cut size.

So when the square is cut, it includes seam allowance and is called the **"unfinished"** measurement.

Once the shape is pieced into a quilt, it will measure ½ inch smaller, which is called the **"finished"** measurement.

Example: A 6-inch block will measure 6 ½ inches square unfinished and 6 inches square finished in the quilt.

As a single, unfinished block, this 9 patch block measures 6 ½ inches

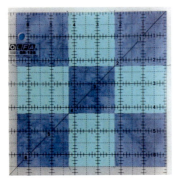

When pieced into a quilt the same square measures 6 inches finished.

This is the fundamental rule of piecing and seam allowance:

Whatever you add, you need to take away exactly.

In order for this simple math to work, all the shapes of your block or quilt first must be cut the correct size with exactly ¼-inch seam allowances added to all sides. We've already learned how to do this in chapter 5.

$$2 + 1/2 = 2\ 1/2$$
$$2\ 1/2 - 1/2 = 2$$

The second step is to take away that ¼-inch seam allowance with every seam you piece. This process of adding and subtracting seam allowance precisely is the core challenge of piecing.

What happens if you cut correctly, but don't piece correctly?

When your ¼-inch seam allowance is off, this simple math will not work. If we sew a bigger than allowed seam allowance (the most common problem), then the blocks will finish up smaller than they were meant to be. If you use a smaller seam allowance, then your blocks will finish up bigger than they were meant to be.

Using a bigger or smaller seam allowance will also affect the integrity of the block itself and your ability to match seams. Remember the lost threads example on page 39 and the impact that small cutting mistake could have to a four patch block? This mistake could just as easily happen in the piecing as the cutting if you're inconsistent in the amount of seam allowance you take away with every seam you stitch.

Piecing math example

This still might not seem like a big deal, so here's a real world example: Sue needs a small quilt to hide an imperfection on her wall. This is a pretty small space, so her quilt needs to finish at exactly 12 ½ by 30 ½ inches in order to cover the problem area, but still fit in the space. She designs the following quilt with 6-inch finished blocks.

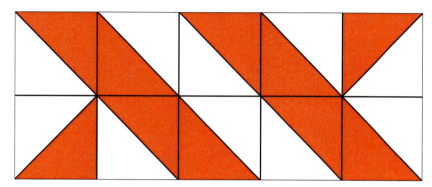

Unfortunately, Sue doesn't piece her blocks accurately or precisely so her triangles don't finish with nice sharp points and the red lines don't match up at all. Instead of sharp lines, they look more like bumpy roads!

Also because she used a very inaccurate seam allowance, her quilt ended up much smaller than she wanted. This is why it's so important to be extremely accurate and precise when piecing your blocks.

ACCURACY AND PRECISION

I'm sure you're wondering - isn't being accurate and precise the same thing? No, they represent two very different ways you can approach a perfect seam.

Accuracy is the ability to hit the target on the bull's eye. In our case accuracy will be sewing an exact ¼-inch seam allowance.

You can actually sew accurately, but without precision. This happens when you sew an exact ¼-inch seam for some seams, but only sporadically through a project.

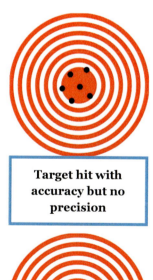

Target hit with accuracy but no precision

Your goal is to hit the bull's eye every time by stitching exactly ¼ inch away from the edges of every piece you sew.

Precision is the ability to hit the same mark repeatedly. In piecing, precision is the ability to cut and sew the same seam every single time.

You can also sew precisely without accuracy. This happens when you sew the same seam allowance through every block, but never take away the accurate ¼-inch seam allowance you need to.

Target hit with precision but no accuracy

Precision is actually more common than accuracy because most of us are very consistent - **consistently off target!**

The challenge is making sure you always sew a straight, accurate ¼-inch seam allowance through the entire seam, every time you sew.

MATCHING SEAMS PERFECTLY

Now that we've learned how to stitch a single seam with both accuracy and precision, let's next learn how to connect two sets of pieced squares together to create a **Two Patch block** with perfectly matched seams.

Start by piecing 2 - 2 ½-inch squares together. Repeat to create a second pieced unit.

Place the two pieced units right sides together and align the edges. Also align the seam lines so the ditch between the pieces lines up perfectly with one unit on top of the other.

1. Pinch the seams together firmly, and then pull back the fabric closest to you to check that the seams are perfectly aligned.

2. Place a pin to the left side of the seam line. If you struggle to insert the pin through the seam allowances, try using thinner pins.

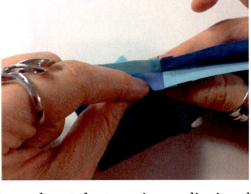

3. Smooth out the two pieces, aligning the corners and stacking the edges right on top of one another.

4. Stitch the two pieces together carefully, making sure to keep the edges aligned with the right edge of the patchwork foot.

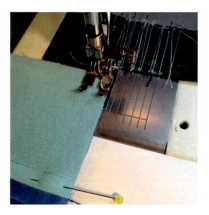

As you stitch near the pin, slow down and pay close attention to the fabrics. They should be in perfect alignment and smooth along the right edge all the way to the pin.

If you instead see the top fabric looking bunchy, like there is more fabric in the top piece than the bottom piece, this is a sign that the fabric pieces either weren't cut the same size (see page 37), or one piece was cut off-grain (see page 15). You can ease in the excess fabric by pulling slightly on the bottom piece. However, if you have too much excess, or tug too hard, this could distort your piece. It's best to stop and rip the seam you're sewing and try again.

Matching Seams Instructions continued

5. Stop stitching before the pin, remove it, and then carefully stitch over the stacked seam allowances.

6. Align the edges and stitch the remainder of the seam, then off onto a scrap charger.

7. Clip the block off the scrap charger and finger press the seam allowances open.

8. Press the block with a hot, dry iron. If the fabrics are light, use a pressing cloth.

Take a close look at the results – do the seam lines match up? Does the block measure exactly 4 ½ inches square? If it doesn't measure this exact size, or the seam lines don't match up, the next step will be figuring out what went wrong along the way.

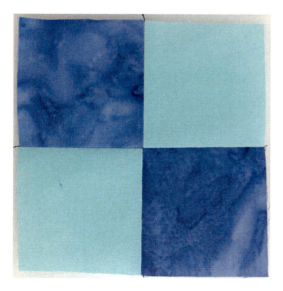
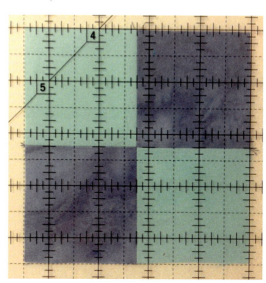

Troubleshooting Mismatched Seams

After piecing any seam that involves matching seam lines, it's important to check that the seams match perfectly. If you don't see a match, the next step is figuring out exactly what went wrong. This is a bit like a mystery you need to solve - what was the culprit behind your mismatched seams?

Top Slipped Down

In this case, the top yellow fabric slipped downward as the seam was pieced.

If the pieces aren't properly pinned, or the pin is removed too soon, the top fabric will easily shift downward as the presser foot puts more pressure on the top fabric.

Remember to pin carefully and securely, and leave the pin in place as long as you can so the seams stay in perfect alignment.

Mismatched Edge

While not as noticeable as a mismatched seam, the mismatched edges are also common. If you start a seam with both edges and corners aligned properly, and both pieces are the same length, then both pieces should finish at the same point, with corners and edges perfectly aligned.

In this case the likely culprit was off grain cutting, which can cause one fabric to "grow" longer than the other past the edge of the block.

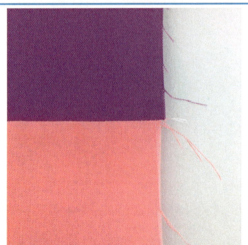

Pleated, not Pretty

Excess fabric bunched up before the pin, and you stitched right over it, which resulted in a pleat or bunched fabric on the surface of the block.

Yes, the seams may match, but this pleat isn't pretty. The likely culprit in this issue is either in the cutting (off grain or shape cut too big) or in the fabric preparation.

Remember, the stiffer the fabric, the easier it will be to control. Try spraying a double layer of starch next time and see how much easier it makes matching seams perfectly.

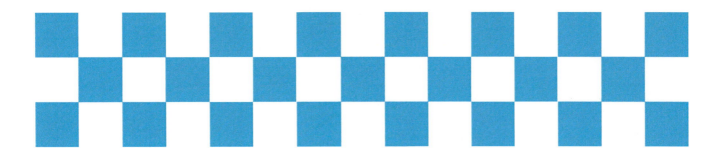

~ Chapter 7 ~
Chain and Strip Piecing

With the basics of machine piecing under our belt, it's time to learn a few time-saving shortcuts. There are methods to speed up the piecing process, and if the fabric is carefully prepared and attention given to every step of the piecing process, then these methods won't be at the expense of accuracy or precision.

In this chapter we will also be able to put all these skills to the test with a simple Basic Blue Nine Patch quilt project. While this project may be simple and small, it covers a wide range of piecing techniques and skills you'll use for every quilt you make.

Chapter 7 Sections:

Chain Piecing - Page 62

Piecing Project: Basic Blue Nine Patch Quilt - Page 63

Strip Piecing - Page 66

To Strip or Not To Strip - Page 70

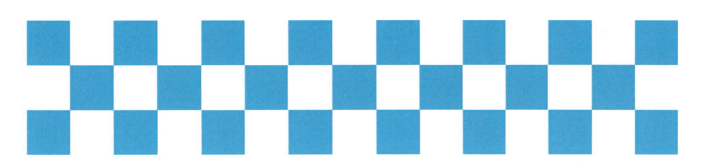

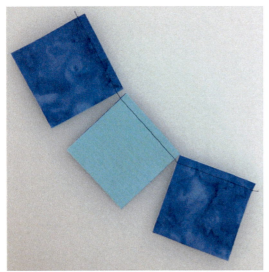

CHAIN PIECING

Chain piecing is one way we can speed up the piecing process by piecing through multiple units at a time with the thread, thus "chaining" all the pieces together.

If you've already been using a scrap charger when you start and end every seam, the process of chain piecing will not be difficult for you to master.

But like any "speedy" method, you need to be careful not to rush or lose your focus. Our goal is still perfect piecing, which requires concentration on stitching the correct seam allowance on every piece, every time.

How to chain piece:

1. Carefully piece two squares of fabric together. Stop with the needle in the down position two stitches off the edge of the fabric.

2. Pick up your next set of squares and slip them under your presser foot right next to the needle. Make sure that the pieces perfectly line up with the right edge of your presser foot.

3. Stitch this seam, then stop again two stitches off the edge of the fabric.

4. Continue until all your fabrics have been pieced. Clip off your scrap charger, sew through it again, and then clip off your chain of blocks.

5. After chain piecing, measure each seam to check the accuracy of your stitching. If any seams are larger or smaller than the required ¼-inch seam allowance, rip those seams and stitch them again.

The first set of squares are still under the foot as you slide in the next set of squares to be stitched

Chain piecing can greatly increase your speed and efficiency as you stitch through a stack of squares, but don't get sloppy or lose your focus!

This technique only works well when you take your time and make sure that each piece is stitched perfectly. Be vigilant in maintaining your accurate ¼-inch seam allowance through every piece, no matter how many you are sewing at a time.

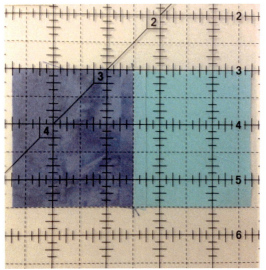

Piecing Project - Basic Nine Patch Quilt

The best way to practice piecing is to piece a real quilt. This project will help you build practical piecing skills into your daily habits, and allow you to see the benefit of properly preparing fabric before cutting.

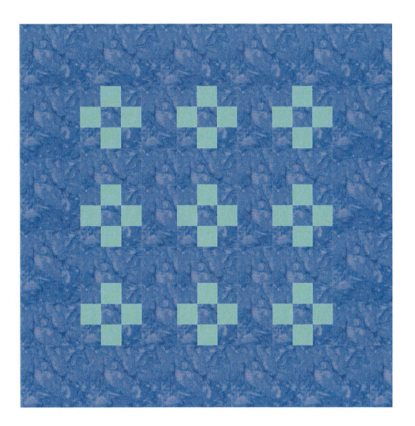

Material List:

½ yard Fabric A (Light Blue)

1 ½ yards Fabric B (Darker Blue)

Cotton Thread to match one fabric color

> **Width-of-Fabric Strips** - This refers to cutting the fabric from selvage to selvage across the width of the fabric.
>
> Width-of-fabric strips are typically 40 to 44 inches long.

Cutting Instructions:

From Fabric A cut 4 width-of-fabric strips 2 ½ inches wide
    Cut 1 strip into 12 – 2 ½ inch squares

From Fabric B cut 4 width-of-fabric strips 2 ½ inches wide.
    Cut 1 strip into 15 – 2 ½ inch squares.

From Fabric B cut 3 width-of-fabric strips 3 ½ inches wide for sashing (page 74).

From Fabric B cut 4 width-of-fabric strips 6 ½ inches wide for borders (page 76).

Piecing Instructions for Basic Nine Patch Quilt

1. Arrange four fabric A squares and five fabric B squares according to the layout below:

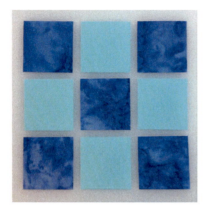

2. Flip the right square over the middle square in each row of the block. Align the right edges so each unit is ready to piece.

3. Following the directions for chain piecing, sew through each fabric pair and then onto the scrap charger to finish.

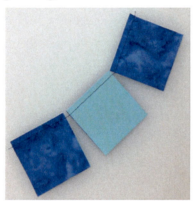

4. Cut the chain apart and measure the seams to check for accuracy. Rip and redo any seams that aren't exactly ¼ inch.

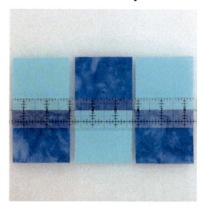

5. Return the pieced units to the block layout. Flip the left squares and repeat the same steps, chain piecing three units together.

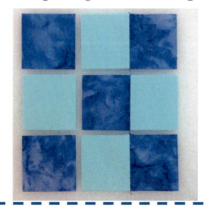

6. Cut the chain apart and finger press all the seams open. Press again with a hot, dry iron to completely flatten the seams.

Leah's Note - *If you stitch VERY slowly you can stitch over your pins, but do this very carefully and with caution. Hitting a pin exactly makes a loud, unpleasant noise, and it can easily damage the bobbin case or needle plate of your machine.*

Piecing Instructions for Basic Nine Patch Quilt continued

7. You should now have three pieced rows. Each row should measure 2 ½ x 6 ½ inches.

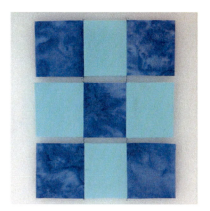

8. Flip the top row over the middle row. With right sides together, align the seam lines and pin as we learned on page 58.

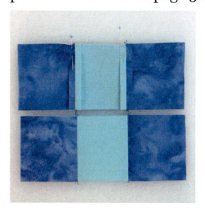

9. Stitch this seam carefully, then open the pieces and check that the seam lines on the right side match perfectly.

10. Repeat steps 8-9 to attach the bottom pieced row to the block. Finger press the seams open, and check the seam lines.

11. If the seams are perfectly matched, press the seams open fully with your iron. The block should measure 6 ½ inches square.

12. Next piece two more Nine Patch blocks with the remaining 2 ½-inch squares to create a total of three blocks.

This will give you plenty of practice chain piecing accurately with a precise ¼-inch seam allowance through every seam.

You'll also get practice at matching seam lines as you piece the three rows of the block together. Make sure to pin carefully before the seam lines and stitch slowly over those areas so the seams match perfectly on the right side of the block.

Once you've mastered the ability to chain piece multiple squares with a perfect ¼-inch seam allowance, you will be ready to simplify this piecing process yet again.

Strip Piecing

Strip piecing simplifies the process of piecing blocks with repeating color patterns. Instead of cutting and piecing with individual small squares, we instead work with long strips, first piecing into strip units, then cutting apart to create a row of pieced squares.

This process speeds up the process of cutting and piecing, but again, it takes effort to incorporate this speedy technique and still maintain our perfect seam allowance. As long as you remain vigilant in the beginning, middle, and end of your seam, you can still stitch very accurately even when strip piecing.

The idea behind strip piecing is very simple; blocks like this Nine Patch can be broken down into two different rows of blocks:

2 Rows of B - A - B squares

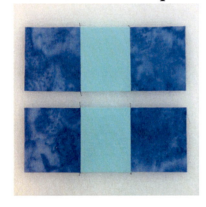

1 Row of A - B - A squares

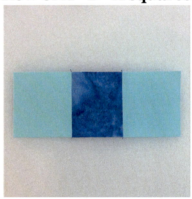

Instead of cutting nine separate squares, piecing the squares into rows, then piecing the rows into a block, this block can be created using two pieced strip sets to create the rows. You'll see how this works as we piece the remaining six blocks of our **Basic Blue Nine Patch Quilt**.

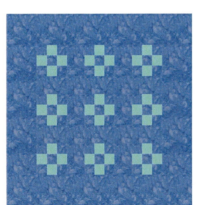

Material List:

To create six Nine Patch blocks and practice strip piecing, you will need the remaining 2 ½-inch wide long fabric strips from both Fabric A and Fabric B.

Find the full material list for the Basic Nine Patch Quilt on page 63.

Strip Piecing Instructions:

> ***Leah's Note*** - Don't obsess about getting the full length of the strip perfectly aligned as long strips often shift as they feed through the machine. Just focus on aligning the right edges along the first 3 inches of the strips to start.
>
> Pinning strips will often make you stretch or pull them out of shape. Avoid pulling on either of the strips as this could easily distort the fabric

1. Place a Fabric A strip and Fabric B strip right sides together and align edges along the right side.

2. Slip the top edge of the strips under your foot and begin stitching with an accurate ¼-inch seam allowance.

Keep the top strip in your left hand so you can easily flip it up and align the right edge with the right edge of the bottom strip.

While the strips may both be around 42 inches long, they may not finish the same length. Don't tug on the strips to force them to fit together perfectly.

Instead allow the feed dogs of the sewing machine to feed the fabric strips under the foot evenly so the resulting pieced strips are flat, straight and square to the grain lines.

3. Once the two strips are pieced, align a second Fabric A strip right sides together with the opposite edge of the Fabric B strip.

4. Sew this seam completely, again making sure to keep the strip edges in perfect alignment without tugging on them.

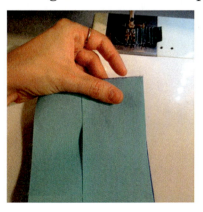

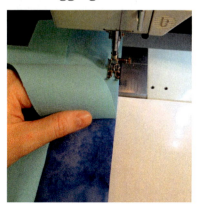

Strip Piecing Instructions continued:

You have now completed one fabric A - B - A strip set.

5. Gently finger press all the seam allowances open down the length of the strips. Press them open and flat with a hot, dry iron.

6. Lay your ruler over the pieced strip set to check the accuracy of your piecing on the middle and two ends of the strip. This pieced strip set should now measure 6 ½ inches wide.

7. If your strips have been pieced properly, the entire length of your three-part strip can be used. Take the strip to your cutting table. Line up horizontal lines on your ruler with the seam lines and square off one end.

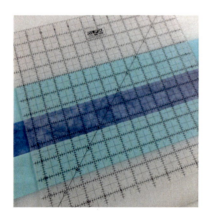

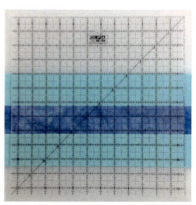

Left-handed first square-up cut

Right-handed first square-up cut

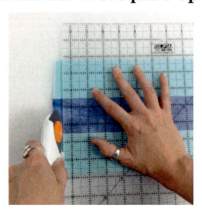

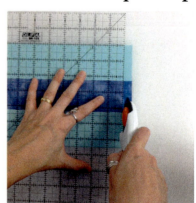

Strip Piecing Instructions continued:

Left-handed cutting rectangles   Right-handed cutting rectangles

8. Flip the strip set over so the squared edge is opposite your dominate hand and cut six rectangular pieces 2 ½ inches wide.

9. Repeat these steps to strip piece a fabric B - A - B strip set.

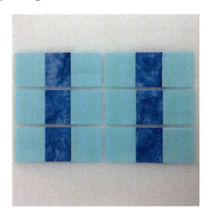 

10. Gently finger press the seams open, then press open fully with your iron. Make sure to double check your piecing by measuring the strip after pressing.

11. From the fabric B - A - B strip set, cut 12 - 2 ½-inch rectangles.

You should now have the following pieces:

6 - A - B - A rectangles

12 - B - A - B rectangles

Using these pieces, lay out three rectangles in the following pattern:

Page 69

Block Piecing Instructions:

To piece your six remaining Nine Patch blocks, follow the instructions on page 65 from step 7.

Pin and carefully match the seam lines, stitch with an accurate ¼-inch seam allowance, and gently finger press the seams open.

You should now have nine Nine Patch blocks that measure exactly 6 ½ inches square.

Now we've created the rest of our blocks in half the time, thanks to strip piecing! In the next chapter we will learn how to connect these blocks together to create our complete Basic Nine Patch Quilt top.

To Strip or Not to Strip

Is strip piecing really a technique you can use even when piecing perfectly? So long as you always work with an accurate and precise seam allowance, strip piecing is a faster method that will reduce the amount of cutting and piecing required for certain types of quilts.

The key to strip piecing is maintaining an accurate seam allowance and not distorting the strips as you piece. Always allow the machine to evenly feed the strips together and focus your attention on keeping the edges aligned with the edge of the presser foot.

With careful handling and precise cutting and piecing, strip piecing can be just as accurate as regular piecing and will save you loads of time as well.

Leah's Note - Early in my quilting journey, I designed this quilt for my mother-in-law.

But when I looked at the pattern, I discovered that I'd designed something that would be very tricky to strip piece. I would have to create multiple strips sets in order to accommodate the piecing.

Instead of simplifying the design or planning the construction with multiple strip sets, I got stubborn. I wanted the quilt to look exactly like the drawn design with no strip piecing.

I ended up paying for this stubborn decision many times over. Piecing this quilt required cutting out all 1,271 - 2 ½-inch squares and then sewing them all back together again!

Lesson Learned - When you can, ALWAYS strip piece!

~ Chapter 8 ~
Piecing a Quilt Top

The ultimate point of everything we've learned so far has been to gain the skill, knowledge, and habits to piece perfect quilts. Most quilts start with blocks, and we've already learned how to piece a simple Nine Patch block, both with chain piecing and strip piecing techniques.

Now let's learn how to piece these blocks together with sashing and borders to finish our first basic quilt top.

Chapter 8 Sections:

Basic Quilt Construction - Page 72

What is Sashing? - Page 73

Piece Sashing Around Blocks - Page 74

Piece a Squared Corner Border - Page 76

Squared Corner Border Variations - 77

Piecing Project - Cornerstone Quilt - Page 78

Piece Sashing with Cornerstones - Page 79

Piece a Cornerstone Border - Page 81

Piece a Mitered Border - Page 82

Mitered Border Variations - Page 85

Calculating Mitered Border Length - Page 85

Basic Quilt Construction

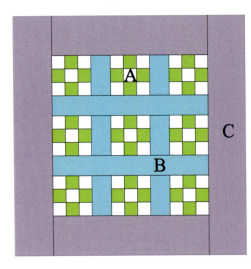

If you remember back in chapter one, the simplest quilts can be broken down into the following sections:

- A – Blocks
- B – Sashing
- C – Borders

Blocks are a popular way to start any quilt as a way to use up fabric, create a pleasing design, and play with interesting shapes and angles.

As we've learned in the previous chapters, you can cut the pieces of a block from yardage or from scraps in your stash.

Sashing is the fabric used to create space between blocks. This negative space acts as a frame around the blocks so you can appreciate them better.

Neat designs are created when blocks are pieced without sashing

Sashing also expands the size of the quilt without adding more complicated piecing to the project. If you've pieced several blocks and just can't stand to piece any more, you can use wide sashing to expand a small number of blocks to create a large quilt.

Borders are also used to expand the surface of your quilt and create a frame around the entire design. Borders can be long strips of the same fabric, or you can piece multiple fabrics together to create very complex borders.

It's important to understand that while our Basic Nine Patch Quilt includes blocks, sashing, and borders, you don't have to have all of these elements in every quilt.

You can piece a quilt entirely with blocks! In this situation the blocks are pieced together with no sashing fabric in between.

This can create interesting quilt designs when the blocks stack against one another. Sometimes you can even create secondary designs by combining two types of blocks together.

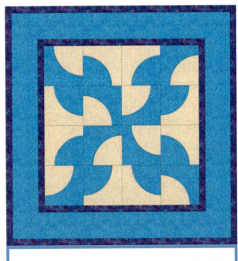

Quilts can also be constructed with just a border around blocks

You can also piece a quilt with just blocks and a border. In this situation the blocks become the artwork inside the big frame of the border.

No matter which quilt blocks you start with, every quilt you make has infinite variety and possibilities.

What is Sashing?

Sashing is the fabric we use to connect our blocks together and expand the size of our quilt. It can also be used to add more negative space around the blocks, which in turn will add more possibilities for piecing or quilting designs.

Two inch sashing is a fairly standard width found in many quilt patterns.

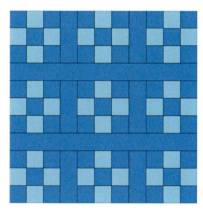

Three inch sashing provides a little more space around the blocks and room for many more quilting designs in this area.

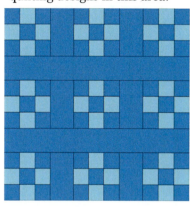

Matching the sashing size to the block size is a great way to super size your quilt with minimal effort.

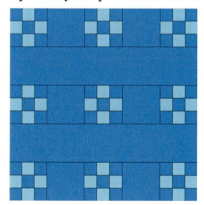

Expanding the sashing in irregular ways can create interesting modern style quilts.

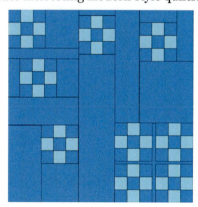

See how different each quilt looks when the width of the sashing is varied?

Most quilters will use 2-inch sashing as a standard in most quilts because it provides a small amount of negative space between the blocks. This is also an easy choice because so many precut fabrics are available in 2 ½-inch strip sets.

Consider piecing with wider sashing instead so you have more space around the blocks and a bigger resulting quilt. While sashing might be the blank areas of a quilt in the piecing, just imagine what you could add to this open canvas with beautiful free motion quilting!

Piece Sashing Around Blocks

Complete Material List found on page 63

Cutting Instructions:

Cut the following pieces from the Fabric B sashing strips:

6 – 3 ½ x 6 ½ inch rectangles

2 – 3 ½ inch width-of-fabric strips

Arrange the sashing strips between the blocks as shown in the photo on the left.

Piecing Instructions:

1. Layer six blocks with 6 - 3 ½ x 6 ½-inch rectangles right sides together. Stitch with an accurate ¼-inch seam allowance.

2. Sew the next seam between the sashing and middle blocks. Then piece the last block to the end to form three-block strips.

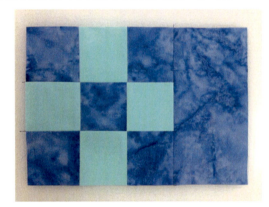

3. Gently finger press all the seam allowances open, then press again with a hot, dry iron to flatten the seams completely.

4. With right sides together, align a sashing strip along the right edge of a block strip and piece together carefully.

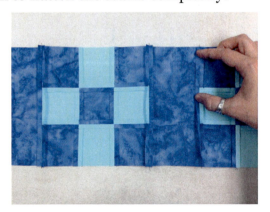

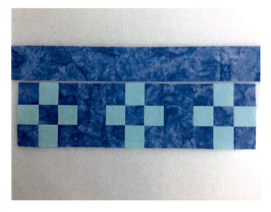

Note: The sashing strips have been intentionally cut longer than the pieced block strip to make it easier to piece. Hold the sashing strip lightly in your left hand and align the right edge with the block strip and allow the machine to feed both layers evenly together.

Sashing Piecing Instructions continued

5. Repeat with the second block and sashing strip. Finger press all the seam allowances open, then press flat with your iron.

6. Square off the edges - With the seams pressed flat, align the seam you've just stitched with a horizontal line on your ruler. Align the edge of the ruler with the edge of the Nine Patch block. Trim off the excess sashing strip that extends beyond the ruler. Repeat with all the sides of the block strips.

Left-handed square-off sashing **Right-handed square-off sashing**

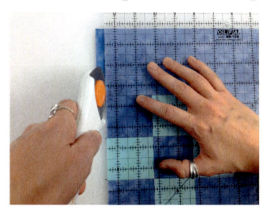
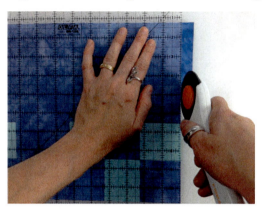

7. With the quilt now in three pieces, it's important to align these units starting from the middle. Fold the top section in half and place a pin to mark the midpoint. Do the same for the other two pieces.

Align the top and middle pieces right sides together, matching the pins that mark the midpoint. Pin to lock the two pieces together. Align the edges carefully and piece with an accurate ¼-inch seam.

Be careful when piecing units like this so you don't stretch or pull on the quilt as you piece. It's easy to distort large pieces of a quilt by handling them roughly. Always be gentle and handle the fabrics with care.

8. Repeat the same steps of finding the midpoint and aligning the edges as you attach the final row of blocks to the quilt top. After stitching this final seam, gently finger press all the seam allowances open, then press again with a hot, dry iron to open and flatten completely.

> ***Leah's Tip:*** A design wall is a terrific addition to any sewing room because it allows you to arrange the blocks on the wall, step back, and view the results from a distance. Easily build a design wall with a piece of 1-inch thick insulation sheeting. Lean this rigid sheeting against your wall and cover with flannel fabric. This fabric will lightly grip your blocks, allowing you to arrange pieces without pinning to the design wall.

Piece a Squared Corner Border

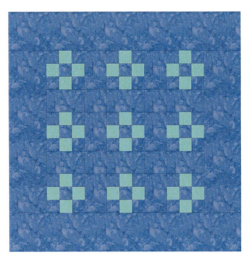

Now it's time to add the border! There are many ways to attach a border to your quilt. This is the simplest method which uses the same straight lines we've been piecing with throughout this book.

Complete Material List found on page 63.

Cutting Instructions:

For this exercise you will need the four Fabric B - 6 ½ inch width-of-fabric strips. Cut two strips 2 inches longer than the quilt top.

Piecing Instructions:

1. Layer the shorter strips along the edges of the quilt, right sides together.

If you've cut your strips long, there should be no need to pin them to the quilt top. Simply layer the border strip on top of the quilt, align the edges so they are stacked perfectly, and allow the fabrics to feed evenly through the machine.

Finger press the seams open and then press again with a hot, dry iron to flatten completely.

2. At your cutting mat, square up the edge of the border by lining up a horizontal line on your ruler with the line you've just stitched, and the edge of the ruler with the edge of the quilt blocks.

Left-handed squaring border edge

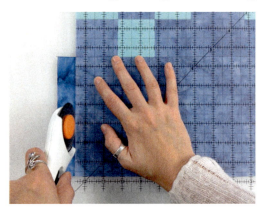

Right-handed squaring border edge

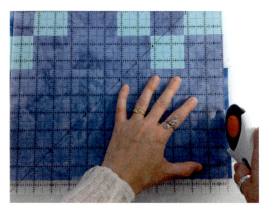

3. Next piece the two remaining border strips to top and bottom edges of the quilt. Gently press all seams open and square off the edges to finish.

SQUARED CORNER BORDER VARIATIONS

You can easily add second or even third borders by simply repeating the same steps. First attach strips to both sides of the quilt, square, then piece strips to the top and bottom edges.

As long as you take the time to square the corners each time you add strips, you can add multiple borders to any quilt top. Play with various widths of borders as well as various colors to create beautiful frames for every quilt you create.

Double border - Add a second round of strips to all sides of the quilt.

Triple border - Add two more rounds of strips to all sides of the quilt.

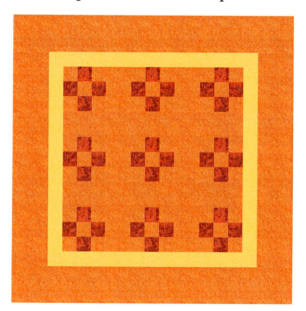 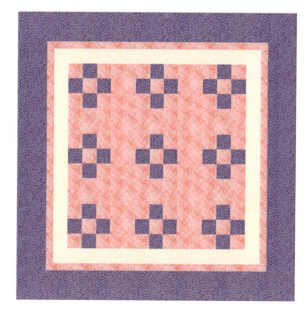

Piecing Project - Cornerstone Quilt

One cool variation for sashing is the addition of cornerstones - small squares located in the intersection of the vertical and horizontal sashing. Since most quilts are created on a grid, it's fun to add cornerstones, or even tiny pieced blocks within the sashing area. These extra squares add more color and design to the quilt.

We will also learn how to attach a cornerstone border to this quilt on page 81.

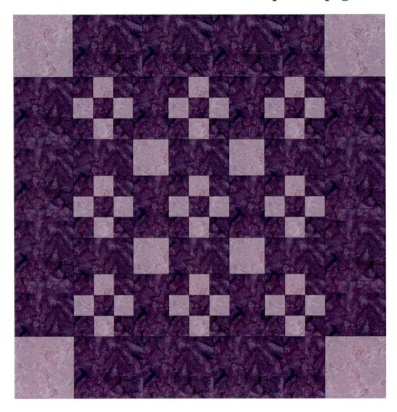

Material List:

2/3 yard Fabric A (Light Purple)

1 ½ yards Fabric B (Darker Purple)

Cotton thread

Fabric Cutting Chart

From Fabric A cut the following:	4 - 2 ½ inch width-of-fabric strips - Blocks
	4 - 3 ½ inch squares - Sashing Cornerstones
	4 - 6 ½ inch squares - Border Cornerstones
From Fabric B cut the following:	5 - 2 ½ inch width-of-fabric strips - Blocks
	12 - 3 ½ x 6 ½ inch rectangles - Sashing Strips
	4 - 6 ½ inch width-of-fabric strips - Borders

Piece Sashing with Cornerstones

Nine Patch Block Piecing Instructions:

Piece nine - Nine Patch blocks using the 2 ½-inch strips and the strip piecing method found on page 66. First piece the following strip units:

1 - A-B-A strip unit and 2 - B-A-B strip units

From these units cut the following:

9 - A-B-A - 2 ½ x 6 ½ inch pieced rectangles

18 - B-A-B - 2 ½ x 6 ½ inch pieced rectangles

Arrange and seam these units together to create nine - Nine Patch blocks.

Cornerstone Sashing Instructions:

1. Follow the sashing instructions on page 74 up to step 3. Set your three block strips aside as you work on your cornerstone sashing.

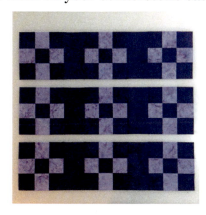

2. Chain piece four Fabric B 3 ½ x 6 ½-inch rectangles to four Fabric A 3 ½-inch squares. Piece two sets of units together.

3. Piece the remaining 3 ½ x 6 ½-inch Fabric B rectangles to the end of the sashing strips. You will now have two pieced strips.

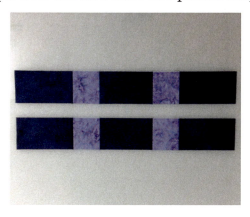

4. Layer a pieced sashing strip over a block strip right sides together, align the edges, and place pins on either side of the seam.

Cornerstone Sashing Instructions continued

5. Repeat step 4 with the second block strip and pieced sashing strip, then align, pin, and piece these two units together.

Double Pin Tip - Place a pin before the point where the seams match and also place a pin slightly after the seam line. This will stop the fabric shifting and ensure a perfect match.

6. Finish by layering the last block strip to the bottom. Pin carefully and piece the final seam.

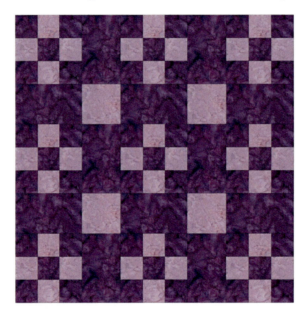

At this point the center of the quilt top is fully pieced. Very gently finger press the seam allowances open, then press again with a hot, dry iron to open and flatten the seams completely.

Piecing sashing with cornerstones is a bit more complicated than piecing without because there are more seams to match.

In this situation your work at cutting and piecing accurately will also be put to the test. If the pieced sashing strip doesn't match with the length of the pieced block strip, obviously something went wrong along the way.

Just remember all the steps to perfect piecing and always handle your fabric gently. With practice aligning and pinning, matching all these seams through the blocks and sashing will soon feel easy and fun.

PIECE A CORNERSTONE BORDER

Cornerstones are not just for sashing - you can also add extra squares, or even extra pieced blocks to the corners of a border.

Again, this requires matching more seams and provides less margin for error than the Squared Corner Border on page 76.

Find the Material List for this quilt on page 78.

Piecing Instructions:

1. Measure the quilt top through the middle using a soft measuring tape and cut the four 6 ½-inch border strips exactly this length.

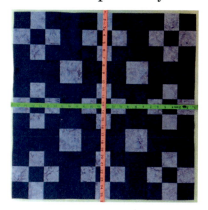

2. Piece strips to the top and bottom of the quilt. Carefully finger press the seams open and then press with a hot, dry iron.

3. Piece two Fabric A 6 ½-inch squares to either side of one border strip. Repeat with the last border strip and squares and gently press all seam allowances open.

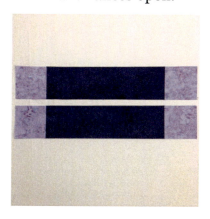

4. Arrange the pieced border strips right sides together with the quilt top. Align and pin the seams, then accurately stitch this seam. Press all seam allowances open.

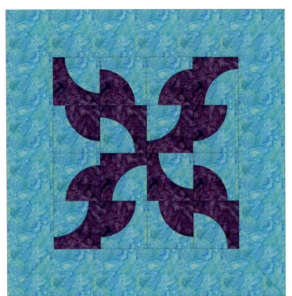

Piece a Mitered Border

If you're looking for a way to seriously spice up your borders, and show off your excellent piecing skills, then you definitely need to learn how to piece with a mitered border which shows your mastery of piecing with a perfect 45-degree seam line through the border corner.

Cutting Instructions:

Refer to page 85 for the formula to calculate the correct width of your border strips.

Piecing Instructions:

1. Fold your quilt top in half to find the midpoint on both sides. Place pins to mark these points. Fold again in the opposite direction so you can mark the midpoint on all sides.

2. Cut your border strips, then fold them and your quilt in half to find the midpoint. Place a pin to mark this point on all strips.

3. Pin each border strip to the quilt top, matching the midpoint pins and smoothing the border strip along the edge. The borders should be longer than the quilt top on all sides as shown below. Be very careful not to stretch your border strips.

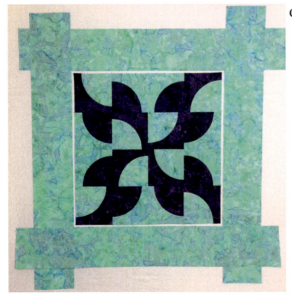

Leah's Note - Mitered corners involve a lot of steps we don't normally take when piecing like backstitching and beginning the seam ¼-inch away from the edge.

Make a note of these differences so you always remember that a mitered border requires a few more steps and more fabric than other border styles.

Mitered Border Instructions continued

4. Start stitching ¼ inch away from the edge of the quilt top. Backstitch to secure. Stitch the length of the seam and stop ¼ inch away from the opposite edge of the quilt top, backstitching again for reinforcement.

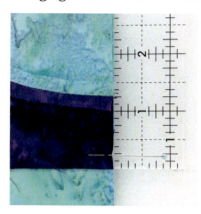

5. Repeat with the remaining border strips. At your pressing board, gently press the seam allowances away from the center of the quilt. With wrong side up, arrange one corner so the border strips form a "+" shape.

6. Using a 12 ½-inch square rotary ruler, line up the 45-degree line with the edge of the border. Align the straight edge of the ruler with the inner quilt top corner.

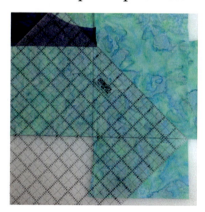

7. Mark the diagonal line from the border stitching to the outside edge with a fabric marking pencil. This will mark your stitching line so it must be marked correctly.

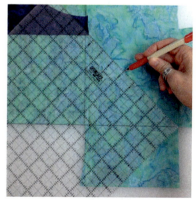

8. Fold the quilt in half diagonally right sides together. Line up the border strips, matching the edges, and pinning along the marked line.

9. At your sewing machine, find the corner point where the two lines of stitching come together. You need to start stitching the seam exactly at this spot.

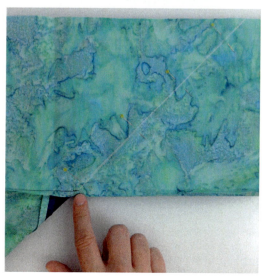

Mitered Border Instructions continued

10. Take three stitches, backstitch, then carefully stitch along the marked line to secure the seam. Stitch slowly and carefully so you don't have to remove pins as you stitch.

11. Open up your seam to check how well it was matched. Make sure to check the corner. If it bubbles or looks bad, rip out the stitches and sew them again.

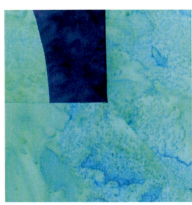

12. Gently finger press the corner mitered seam open, then press again with your iron to set in the seam. This is a bias seam so be very gentle with the fabric as you press.

13. The corner where the border meets the quilt can be a difficult area. Fold down the seam allowance and press the diagonal lines from the border flat.

14. Carefully trim the excess fabric on either side of the miter. At this point you can press the seam between the quilt interior and border open, carefully flattening the many layers in the corners of the quilt.

Repeat steps 5 through 13 to mark and stitch each corner with a mitered seam.

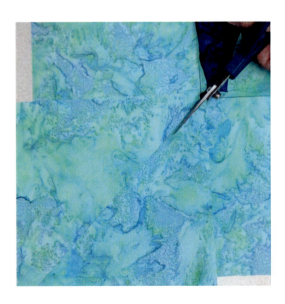

Mitered Corner Border Variations

You can also add additional strips to a mitered border for an enhanced effect for the corners of your quilts. This looks especially beautiful with striped fabrics, though the process of matching up strips can be a challenge!

To attach a multi-level mitered corner border, you first need to piece all the strips together into rows. By piecing all the various strips together at the beginning, you will only need to stitch one mitered seam for each corner and if properly executed, the seams of each strip will match up perfectly.

Really show off your piecing skills by piecing multiple strips together and matching all corner seams!

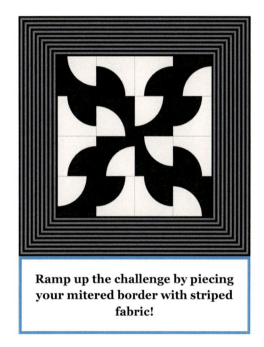

Ramp up the challenge by piecing your mitered border with striped fabric!

Calculating Miter Border Length

As you can see, mitered corners require a lot more fabric to properly align the diagonal seam through the corner. The last thing you want to do is start piecing a border strip only to find it's too short to align the corner properly.

You can use the following formula to determine the length of strips for any quilt.

(width of border x 2) + width or length of quilt top + 5 inches = length of strips

Example: If your border is 5 inches wide and being attached to a quilt that's 55 inches square, you will need strips that measure 70 inches long.

You need to have double the width of the border, plus an extra 5 inches for leeway. Again, it's always a good idea to work with more fabric than you need, especially when piecing mitered corners!

~ Chapter 9 ~
Let's Piece Triangles!

Up until now, we've worked entirely with squares and rectangles, which can create an amazing variety of blocks and quilt designs.

But what if you wanted to piece a star block? It's simply not possible to piece a star with only square and rectangular shapes!

In order to piece a star, we need to be able to piece sharp angles to create the beautiful sharp points of this block. In this chapter we will learn how to piece Half Square Triangles and Flying Geese and explore two interesting quilt projects, plus many beautiful blocks we can piece with these unique units.

Chapter 9 Sections:

Half Square Triangles - Page 87

Piecing Half Square Triangles - Page 88

Calculating Half Square Triangles - Page 90

Piecing Project - Chocolate Cookie Quilt - Page 91

Troubleshooting Half Square Triangle Issues - 94

Flying Geese - Page 95

Piecing Flying Geese - Page 96

Piecing Project - Flying Geese Diamond Quilt - Page 98

Troubleshooting Flying Geese Issues - Page 101

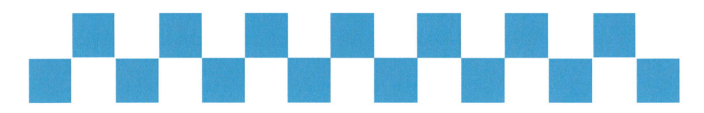

Half Square Triangles

The name of these triangles is quite odd. Half square? What does that mean?

Half square simply means that these triangles are made by using half of a square. This makes for a triangle that has the same length on two sides and is a staple of many quilting traditional quilt blocks.

These blocks are created using two squares, sewing on either side of the middle seam, and then cutting them apart. You will make two Half Square Triangles for every set of squares you piece.

> **Leah's Note -** *You will commonly find Half Square Triangles noted in quilt patterns with the abbreviation HST.*

Does this look intimidating? Fortunately, quilters have found many ways to make triangle piecing easier.

Back before we had rotary cutters, quilters would cut out triangles individually with scissors and templates. Working with the actual triangle shape can be challenging because the center diagonal seam, the hypotenuse, is on the bias.

Remember back from our discussion about grain line from Chapter 2? The bias is the most stretched part of the seam which is really hard to handle when being pieced.

Fortunately we no longer have to cut and piece individual triangles. We can easily piece this shape using two squares instead, so you're never actually working with a triangle shape.

By using squares to piece our triangles, rather than actual triangle shapes, we're able to control this stretchy bias seam much easier. Even still, be mindful of sewing and even marking the diagonal of a square; if you're too rough with your fabric, you can easily distort it out of shape.

It's also a good idea to heavily starch the fabric you plan to use for half square triangles. Stiffer fabric will be far easier to control and result in perfectly straight piecing lines which in turn will make perfectly straight diagonal seams for your half square triangles.

> *Always starch your fabric twice when piecing triangles!*

Piecing Half Square Triangles

Let's learn how to piece half square triangles! Grab some scrap fabric and get ready to master this fun triangle shape.

Cutting Instructions:

Cut one 3 ¼ inch square from Fabric A

Cut one 3 ¼ inch square from Fabric B

Piecing Instructions:

1. On the wrong side of one square, carefully mark a diagonal line from point to point using a fabric marking pencil.

2. Next measure ¼ inch to the right of the center line and mark again. Repeat measuring and marking to the left of center as well.

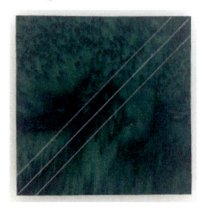

3. Layer the Fabric A square on top of the Fabric B square, right sides together with the marked side facing you. Make sure the edges of the squares are perfectly aligned.

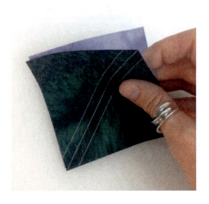

4. Slip the stacked squares under the foot and align the needle with the marked line on the far right. Stitch exactly on top of this marked line from corner to corner.

Piecing Half Square Triangles Continued

5. Stitch through a scrap charger and clip off the squares. Rotate the squares and stitch again along the outer marked line.

6. After stitching, measure the distance from the two lines of stitching. They should be exactly ½-inch apart and perfectly straight.

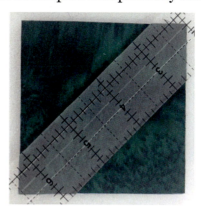

7. Using your rotary cutter or a pair of scissors, cut the blocks apart along the center marked line.

8. Gently finger press the seam allowances open, then take the HSTs to your pressing board to press with a hot, dry iron.

Cut down to the exact size – Half square triangles can be tricky to piece to an exact size. After many years of fussing with this shape, I found it was actually easier to cut the starting squares bigger, then trim the finished half square triangles to the exact size I needed.

Lay your ruler over both blocks, lining the diagonal line with the diagonal seam line on the HST. Trim the side. Rotate 90 degrees and trim a second side.

Now line up the two cut edges with the 2 ½-inch marks on the ruler, and the diagonal line in the center. Take your time to make sure all three marks line up exactly, then trim the excess from the two remaining sides.

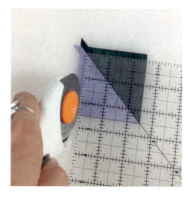

Visibility is key - If you can't see the diagonal pieced line on the half square triangle through your rotary ruler, you will not be able to line up the shape and trim it down accurately. Most piecing issues with half square triangles come from working with an inaccurately cut shape. If the shape doesn't start correctly, it will never piece the correct size.

CALCULATING HALF SQUARE TRIANGLES

What if you wanted to change the blocks in our Basic Blue Nine Patch quilt for blocks with half square triangles? How would you calculate the size of squares to start with?

To calculate the size of your half square triangles, simply use this formula:

Finished HST size + 7/8" = size to cut

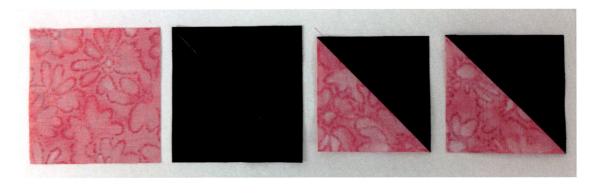

Example - If you needed half square triangles to finish at three inches square, you will cut 3 7/8-inch squares to start.

After sewing the squares along the diagonal, and cutting them apart, the resulting half square triangles will measure 3 ½ inches (the unfinished measurement), and when pieced on all sides, they will measure 3 inches finished.

While this is the standard calculation for half square triangles, it's quite tricky to cut 7/8 inch measurement accurately. It's far easier to cut the square larger – 4 ¼ inches in this case.

Then the resulting half square triangles will be larger and you can easily trim them down to the exact size they need to be for your pattern.

Leah's Note - I prefer to give myself more wiggle room when calculating HSTs. I use the following formula, then carefully trim the shapes down to the exact required size.

Finished size + 1 ¼ inches = size to cut

Yes, using this calculation will waste a bit more fabric, but it's worth it to have a slightly bigger half square triangle you can trim down precisely.

Piecing Project - Chocolate Cookie Quilt

Let's now practice making half square triangles with this fun quilt project!

Material List:

1 1/3 yard Fabric A (Dark Brown)

1 yard Fabric B (Beige)

Cotton thread to match one fabric

Fabric Cutting Chart

From Fabric A cut the following:	4 - 2 ½ inch width-of-fabric strips - Blocks 4 - 6 ½ inch width-of-fabric strips - Borders 2 – 4 ¼ inch squares - Small HSTs 4 - 3 ½ x 6 ½ inch rectangles - Sashing 2 – 7 1/4 inch squares - Large HSTs
From Fabric B cut the following:	5 - 2 ½ inch width-of-fabric strips - Blocks 2 – 4 ¼ inch squares - Small HSTs 8 - 3 ½ x 6 ½ inch rectangles - Sashing 2 – 7 1/4 inch squares - Large HSTs

Chocolate Cookie Quilt Piecing Instructions:

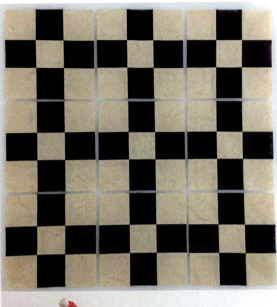

Nine Patch Block Piecing Instructions:

Piece nine - Nine Patch blocks using the 2 ½ inch strips and the strip piecing method we learned on page 66. Piece the following strip units:

1 - A-B-A strip unit and 2 - B-A-B strip units

From these units cut the following:

9 - A-B-A - 2 ½ x 6 ½ inch pieced rectangles

18 - B-A-B - 2 ½ x 6 ½ inch pieced rectangles

Arrange and seam these units together to create nine - Nine Patch blocks.

Piece small half square triangles

Piece two sets of half square triangles using the Fabric A and B 4 ¼-inch squares. Stitch and trim to create 4 - 3 ½ inch half square triangles.

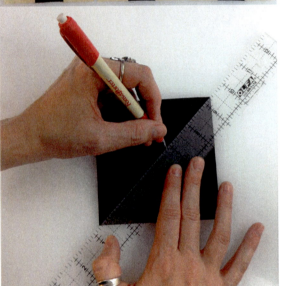

Piece large half square triangles

Piece two sets of half square triangles using the Fabric A and B 7 ¼-inch squares. Stitch and trim to create 4 – 6 ½ inch half square triangles.

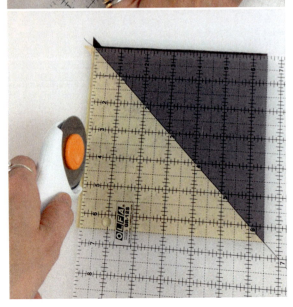
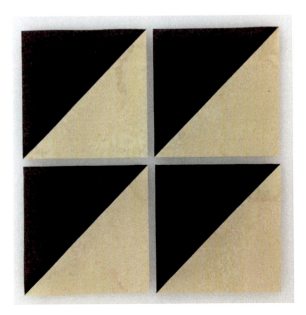

Chocolate Cookie Quilt Piecing Instructions continued:

Arrange the pieces of the quilt according to the photo below. Note the color placement of the 3 ½ x 6 ½ inch sashing strips.

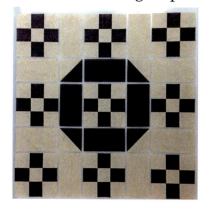

Piece the blocks into strips with sashing rectangles, then piece the sashing and small HSTs into strips.

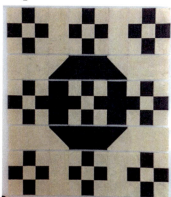

Review the directions on page 79 on piecing sashing with cornerstones. Match all the seams and pin carefully before you stitch.

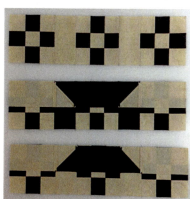

Press the seams open, and measure the quilt top through the middle.

Cut the Fabric A 6 ½-inch width-of-fabric strips to length, then piece two large HSTs to both ends of two strips.

Piece the two plain strips to the sides of the quilt top. Press seams open. Finally attach the pieced border strips to the top and bottom edges, making sure to pin carefully to match the seams in the corners.

Review this method on page 81 for piecing a cornerstone border.

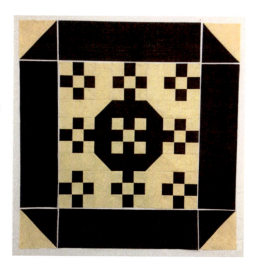

Troubleshooting Half Square Triangles

As you piece your half square triangle into blocks or quilts, be on the lookout for the following common issues that crop up with this shape.

Diagonal Points Don't Match

In this case, one side is significantly off the mark, which indicates it either slipped out of position while piecing, or it was cut incorrectly to start.

Try again and double check your shape is accurately cut with the diagonal seam running exactly from one corner to the other.

Also make sure the edges of the pieces stay in perfect alignment as you sew over the seam lines. Leave the pin in place as long as you can to keep the fabrics from shifting.

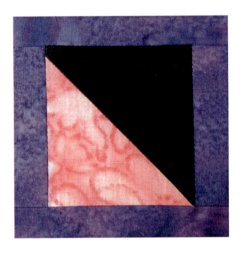

Floating Point

The point of these triangles is supposed to reach exactly to the edge of the next piece. If you find a point floating off in space, it is a sign the half square triangle was not cut down properly after piecing.

It's also a sign that less than a ¼-inch seam allowance was used to piece this seam. Try again and be sure to maintain an accurate and precise seam allowance all the way through the seam.

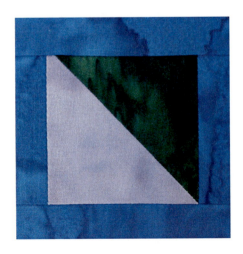

Blunted Point

Points are supposed to be pointy!

If you find your half square triangle points blunted on the end, this is another sign the triangle wasn't trimmed down properly after piecing.

It's also a sign that more than a ¼-inch seam allowance was used to piece the seam. Try again and make sure to keep the fabric edges perfectly aligned with the edge of the presser foot.

Flying Geese

The next triangle we will learn to piece is the flying geese block. This is an extremely versatile block that can be used in a variety of ways when piecing quilts.

Just like the half square triangles, flying geese are not pieced using triangle shapes, which might be tricky to cut and piece accurately.

Instead this traditional quilt shape is created using two squares and one rectangle. By carefully stitching and flipping over the squares, you can create two right triangles in both corners of the rectangular shape.

If pieced accurately, you should have three points to every flying geese unit - the two corners and point where the squares overlap in the center.

The background rectangle of the flying geese unit is the most important element of this unit because it provides structure and stability to this shape.

So long as the rectangle is cut properly, and both squares are stitched along the diagonal properly, the resulting triangle shape should finish perfectly. The key is keeping the background rectangle intact so you can always trust these edges to be straight and true.

Fabric selection tip - The background rectangle will remain in our flying geese, and could potentially show through the light fabric pieced on top.

When picking colors for flying geese units pick a darker color for the squares and a lighter color for the background rectangle so it will not show through.

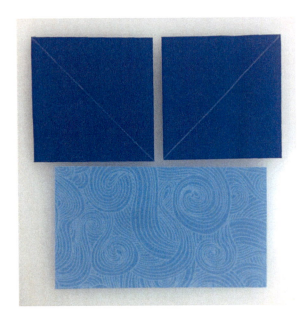

Piecing Flying Geese

Let's piece one flying geese unit. Flying geese always finish as a rectangular unit where the length is double the width. Unlike half square triangles, we can will only piece one unit at a time.

Cutting Instructions:

2 - 2 ½ inch squares in Fabric A

1 – 2 ½ x 4 ½ inch rectangle in Fabric B

Piecing Instructions:

1. Using a ruler and marking pencil, carefully mark a diagonal line from corner to corner on the wrong side of the squares.

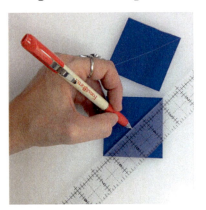

2. Align one square, right sides together, with one side of the rectangle, matching the edges and two corners on one side.

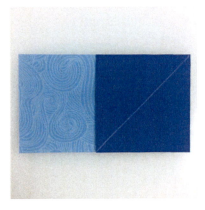

3. Stitch from corner to corner, staying precisely on top of the marked line.

4. Finger press the fabric from the middle to the outer corner and check that the edges of the fabric meet the edges of the rectangle.

Piecing Flying Geese Instructions continued

5. Using scissors, cut away the fabric below the top triangle. This unneeded piece will add extra bulk to your quilt if left in place.

Do not cut the background rectangle. So long as this piece stays intact, you will be able to piece a perfect flying geese unit.

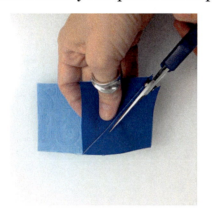

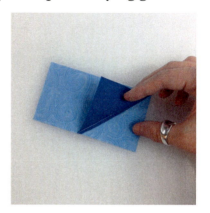

6. Press the first triangle with a hot dry iron to flatten the seam.

7. Line up the second square in the opposite corner of the rectangle and stitch on the marked diagonal line.

8. Repeat finger pressing the triangle over and cutting away the excess fabric on the bottom part of the triangle.

9. Give the flying geese unit a final press to flatten the seams. If any fabric extends beyond the background rectangle, square it off carefully with your rotary cutter.

Piecing Project - Flying Geese Diamond Quilt

Let's practice piecing flying geese units with this simple variation of our Basic Nine Patch Quilt. Again, we're working with the same Nine Patch quilt blocks, but making subtle changes to the sashing and borders to create a beautiful new design.

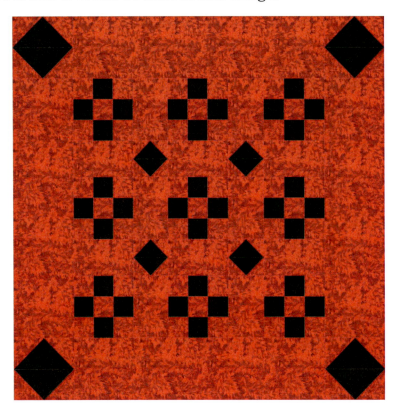

Material List:

½ yard Fabric A (Black)

1 3/4 yards Fabric B (Red)

Cotton thread to match Fabric B

Fabric Cutting Chart

Fabric A	4 - 2 ½ inch width-of-fabric strips - Blocks
	8 - 3 ½ x 2 inch rectangles - Small Flying Geese
	8 - 3 ½ x 6 ½ inch rectangles - Large Flying Geese
From Fabric B:	5 - 2 ½ inch width-of-fabric strips - Blocks
	16 - 2 inch squares - Small Flying Geese Squares
	16 - 3 ½ inch squares - Large Flying Geese Squares
	12 - 3 ½ x 6 ½ inch rectangles - Sashing
	4 - 6 ½ inch width-of-fabric strips - Borders

9 Patch Block Piecing Instructions:

Piece nine - Nine Patch blocks using the 2 ½-inch strips and the strip piecing method we learned on page 66. First piece the following strip units:

1 - A-B-A strip unit and 2 - B-A-B strip units

From these units cut the following:

9 - A-B-A - 2 ½ x 6 ½ inch pieced rectangles

18 - B-A-B - 2 ½ x 6 ½ inch pieced rectangles

Arrange and seam these units together to create nine -Nine Patch blocks.

Small flying geese

Piece the 16 Fabric B 2 inch squares with the 8 Fabric A 3 ½ x 2 inch rectangles to create eight small flying geese units.

Piece two small flying geese units together to create a 3 ½ inch unfinished Square-in-a-Square block. Repeat with the remaining flying geese to create four small blocks.

Larger flying geese

Piece the 16 Fabric B 3 ½ inch squares and 8 Fabric A 6 ½ x 3 ½ inch rectangles to make eight large flying geese units.

Piece two larger flying geese units together to create a 6 ½ inch unfinished Square-in-a-Square block. Repeat with the remaining flying geese to create four large blocks.

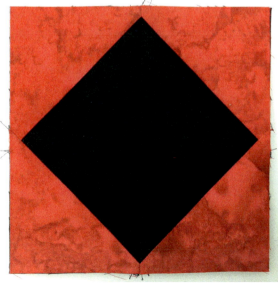

Flying Geese Diamond Quilt Piecing Instructions continued

1. Now it's time to put it all together! Arrange the pieces to match the picture below:

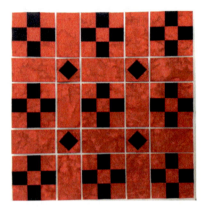

2. Piece the blocks into strips, and piece the sashing and small Square-in-a-Square blocks into strips. Connect the pieced block and sashing strips to create the quilt top.

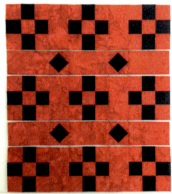

3. Review the directions on page 79 on piecing sashing with cornerstones. Make sure to match all the seams and pin carefully before you stitch. Press the seams open carefully.

4. Measure the quilt top, then cut the Fabric A 6 ½ inch width-of-fabric strips to this length. Piece two large Square-in-a-Square blocks to both ends of two strips.

5. Piece the two plain strips to the sides of the quilt top. Press seams open.

6. Finally attach the pieced border strips to the top and bottom edges, making sure to match the seams in the corners.

Troubleshooting Flying Geese Issues

Flying geese units can have the same piecing issues as half square triangles (page 94), and it's important to understand why an issue is happening. Sometimes knowing where you're going wrong is all it takes to correct the issue and suddenly you'll be able to piece that triangle shape perfectly every time.

Asymmetrical Triangles

If you happen to notice one triangle looks bigger than the other, this is a sure sign either the lines were marked incorrectly or the pieces were cut incorrectly.

Make sure to mark the squares of every flying geese unit as precisely as possible from corner to corner. When aligning the square on top of the rectangle, take extra time to ensure the edges and two corners are stacked right on top of one another.

Also be on the lookout for shifting! If the square or rectangle shift as you piece, stop and get back on track before proceeding. There's no point in completing a seam if it shows clear early signs of being incorrectly aligned.

Floating Point

The point of both triangles should reach to the seam line when pieced to other shapes. If they don't, this is a sign you didn't stitch exactly on the marked line as you pieced your flying geese unit.

It might be the distance of one thread of fabric, but as we've learned many times, this is enough to cause major issues for quilt piecing.

Consistency is the key! Stitch exactly on the line for every seam and both triangles will finish the same size and length.

The Cross is Showing

If this cross where the two triangles overlap is showing on the right side of the block, this means you didn't piece with an accurate ¼-inch seam allowance. Your seam was a bit narrow, which means the overall shape will be slightly bigger than it should be.

This area does tend to be thick and bulky because of all the seam allowances. Make sure to place a pin before and after this spot to ensure it stays in position and aligned properly with the pieces it's being stitched to.

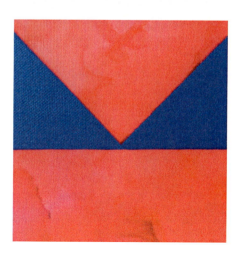

Page 101

~ Chapter 10 ~
Piecing Weird Shapes

With two cool triangles under your belt, we're definitely ready to tackle piecing even more fun shapes. These shapes sometimes have unique rules governing how they are pieced, how the seam allowances are pressed, and how the shape connects with other shapes.

Many shapes, like curves, appear intimidating, but do keep in mind that these have been used to piece beautiful quilts for over one hundred years, and without the aid of handy tools like rotary cutters or even sewing machines.

In this chapter we will learn how to piece hexagons flowers by hand and traditional curved seam blocks by machine. Ultimately no matter how it's pieced, the most important detail is making sure you're always stitching with an accurate and precise ¼-inch seam allowance through every seam, every time.

Chapter 10 Sections:

Piecing Templates - Page 103

Cutting Hexagons Using Templates - Page 104

Cutting Shapes with a Die Cutting Machine - Page 105

Piecing Hexagon Flowers by Hand - Page 106

Hexagon Seam Allowances - Page 108

Shortcut Hexagon Flowers by Machine - 109

Curved Seam Piecing - Page 110

Piecing Project - Drunkard's Path Quilt - Page 112

Troubleshooting Curved Seams - Page 114

Piecing Templates

Flying geese and half square triangles are easy to cut and piece because they're created using simple squares and rectangles. You can also chain piece these triangle units which make them very quick to produce.

There are shapes, however, that cannot be speed pieced with chain piecing. These shapes include diamonds, equilateral triangles, hexagons, and curved pieces.

These shapes are cut using templates. You can make your own homemade templates by tracing a shape on thicker material, either template plastic or cardboard, and cutting it out the exact size of the shape you need with seam allowance included.

> ***The most important rule for odd shapes - they must be cut exactly the right size in order to piece perfectly together.***

The downside to homemade templates is they cannot be easily cut with a rotary cutter. It's very easy to nick the edges of the template and over time, nick after nick will slowly shrink the size of your cut shape, and equally shrink your chances of piecing the shapes perfectly.

You can also purchase template sets made from thick acrylic that can be cut using your regular rotary cutter.

> **Leah's Note -** *I've made many templates myself and found that the job is not only difficult, it's a waste of time.*
>
> *High quality acrylic templates are available in just about any size and shape you can think of and for any type of quilt.*

The benefits of acrylic templates are many: they can't be nicked by your rotary cutter, they're firm and rigid just like your normal cutting rulers, and they've been precisely engineered so that they produce perfectly shaped blocks when pieced accurately.

Many challenging quilt designs like the Double Wedding Ring, Grandmother's Flower Garden, and Lone Star have template sets made specifically for them. It's far easier to create these quilts with an acrylic template set created to produce those blocks at the exact right size.

Cutting Hexagons Using Templates

Hexagons, or hexies as many quilters now like to call them, are a super popular shape to piece, not just by machine, but also by hand. Let's cut the pieces for one flower block using the Small Hexagon Set G by Marti Michell.

Cutting Instructions:

1. First measure the 2-inch template from side to side to find the width. This template measures slightly less than 4 inches wide.

2. The next step is to prepare our fabric, starch and press twice, and then cut strips 4 inches wide.

3. Align the template on the fabric strip, making sure the sides perfectly align to the top and bottom edges of the strip.

4. Carefully cut along the angles. Rotate the fabric around for the cuts on the side opposite your dominant hand.

Because this template was slightly smaller than the 4 inch strip we cut, make sure to trim the top edge of the template as well so the fabric shape matches the template shape perfectly.

Continue cutting hexagons from the strip of fabric, making sure to double check the alignment of the template on the fabric. If the template shifts while cutting, do not use the resulting incorrect shape. Shift your template and cut again more accurately.

> **Leah's Note -** *To stabilize the template, cut a piece of **InvisiGrip** and cover the wrong side of the template. This clear gripping material will ensure the template doesn't shift so you can cut accurately through the entire strip.*

Cutting Shapes with a Die Cutting Machine

Templates have long been used to cut shapes like hexagons, but yes, this is a multi-step process that can be both time-consuming and tedious for a big quilt.

Recently die-cutting machines like the AccuQuilt Go! have enabled quilters to cut tricky shapes like hexagons quickly and easily using foam covered dies.

However, even though using a machine like this saves time, you still need to be vigilant with proper fabric preparation and focus on grain line.

How to cut hexagons with an AccuQuilt Go die:

1. Place a ruler over the die you plan to use and mark a line ¼ inch to the top and bottom of the blade. This line will help you line up your fabric on grain so the die will cut with the grainline of the fabric.

2. Measure the distance between the two marked lines. This measurement is how wide you need to cut your strips.

3. Prepare your fabric by prewashing, starching and pressing, then add a little more stability by starching a second time. This second layer of starch will help the fabric stay flat and not slip off the lines and off grain.

4. Line up the edge of the strip with the line you've marked on the die. If the strip is long, you can fold it so up to 4 layers of fabric rest on top of the hexagon shape. Make sure the fabric extends to fully cover the shape on all sides.

5. Place the cutting mat on top of the die and press down as you feed the die into the AccuQuilt machine.

6. In one pass, you can cut up 4 hexagons! This greatly speeds up the process of cutting this shape, and ensures it will be cut exactly the right size every time.

Precut Hexagons

If you're really looking for a shortcut to piecing hexagons, definitely keep your eyes peeled for these precut hexagon packs at your local quilt shop. These sets of hexies are laser cut and include a marking template to mark the dots in the corners of each shape.

Just remember the one downside to precuts – the inability to prewash this fabric. In the end, after the quilt is pieced, quilted, and washed, it will finish with a crinkled, wrinkled appearance on the surface as the cotton fabric relaxes and shrinks to its finished size.

Piecing Hexagon Flowers by Hand

Hexagons are an interesting shape that is actually easier to piece by hand than by machine because you do not stitch into the seam allowance of the hexagon shape, but rather from the exact points the seam allowance starts (dot to dot).

Piecing hexagons into flowers is a popular way to create a Grandmother's Flower Garden quilt. Cut out several flowers and you'll have a fun hand piecing project to take with you anywhere!

Cutting Instructions:

1 hexagon for the middle (yellow)

6 hexagons for the 1st ring (Purple)

12 hexagons for the 2nd ring (Green)

Piecing Instructions:

1. The templates we used to cut our hexies on page 104 have a special feature – small holes cut out of each corner which allow you to easily dot where the stitching line should start and finish for every seam.

If your template or die doesn't feature these holes, line up a ruler with the edge of the hexagon shape and draw lines ¼ inch away from the edges. You need to be able to see an accurate line to piece along this edge.

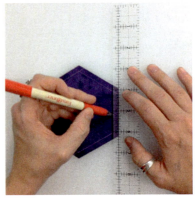

2. Align the middle hexagon with a first ring hexagon right sides together, and insert your needle in a corner dot. Make sure the needle is piercing through the middle of the dots marked on both fabrics.

Take a tiny stitch and loop around to where you first inserted your needle to create a back stitch to secure this start.

Hexagon Flower Instructions continued

3. Make tiny stitches along the edge of the hexagon exactly ¼ inch from the edge of the shape. For hand piecing you also need to maintain even, tiny stitches down the seam.

4. When you reach the dot in the next corner, insert your needle in the center of the dot, then swing back to back stitch and secure the end. Tie a knot and cut your thread.

5. Hand piece two more first ring hexagons to the middle hexagon so it matches the photo below:

6. Piece the remaining hexagons of the first ring by setting in the shape along all three sides of the hexagon adjacent to it. Starting on one side, stitch dot to dot to reach the center hexagon.

7. Backstitch to secure the area where all the hexagons join, then stitch across the center hexagon dot to dot to reach the opposite side. Backstitch again, then finish off by stitching the last dot to dot segment.

8. With the first ring finished, arrange the second ring the same way – piece every other hexagon first, then insert hexagons in the open spaces, stitching all three seams in one go.

> **Leah's Note** - Hand piecing is a terrific way to get familiar with a ¼-inch seam. By either marking the entire seam line, or by eyeballing the line between the dots, you will soon be able to judge this measurement by eye. It's a useful skill for any perfect piecer to build!

Hexagon Seam Allowances

Because of the unique angles and many sides of the hexagon shape, this is one of the few shapes that requires you to press the seam allowances to one side rather than open. The reason for this is the connection point where the three seams come together. Pressing the seams open will cause issues at this major intersection.

However, when pressed to one side, the fabric in the seam allowances will magically fan open, creating a beautiful, flat intersection shown in the photo on the left.

Pieced Hexies Craftsy Class

Did you know there are multiple methods for hand piecing hexagon shapes? For even more interesting ideas to piece hexagons using English paper piecing, definitely check out the Craftsy class **Pieced Hexies** taught by Mickey Depre.

In this class you will learn the basics of English paper piecing, plus discover Mickey's method for piecing the hexagon shape with multiple fabrics to create even more variations within the design.

Learn more about Pieced Hexies at Craftsy.com

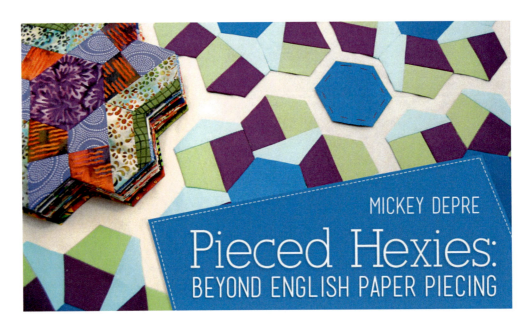

Shortcut Hexagon Flowers by Machine

If you're short on time, hate hand piecing, or simply needed to produce a large Grandmother's Flower Garden quilt LAST week for your daughter's wedding, it might be a good idea to take a shortcut.

The shortcut is to bypass the hexagon shape altogether and slice it in half. This half-hexagon shape can be cut with either templates or dies, and it will enable you to quickly piece by machine from the edges of the shape rather than from dot to dot.

By cutting the hexagon in half you will be able to use both chain piecing and strip piecing, making this method much, much faster.

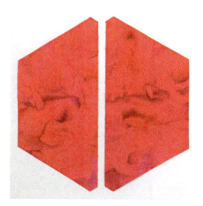

Cutting Instructions:

2 half hexagons for the middle (yellow)

12 half hexagons for the first ring (Pink)

24 half hexagons for the second ring (Green)

46 half hexagons for the background (Navy)

Piecing Instructions:

1 Arrange the cut half hexagon shapes to create the flower block design. You will need a large table to arrange all the pieces in rows.

2. Begin piecing the half hexagons together along the short sides of the shape, which will create a long strip of half hexagons. Make sure to keep the colors in the correct arrangement as you piece the shapes together.

3. Once the rows are pieced, align them right sides together, match the seam lines, pin, and piece carefully down the length of the strip.

4. Press the seams open and check they match perfectly. Continue piecing all the rows together in the same manner.

In this way you can greatly speed up the process of piecing hexagons by machine. However, these hexagons will have a noticeable seam line running through the middle of each shape. Reduce the appearance of this seam by using solid or solid reading fabrics like batiks which will hide the extra seam line from a distance.

Even though this is a shortcut method, you'll still need to remain vigilant to maintain your accurate ¼-inch seam allowance. Preparing the fabric from the start with a double layer of starch will also greatly reduce the stretch in the diagonal sides of the hexagons.

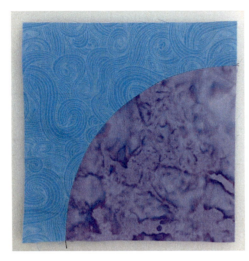

Curved Seam Piecing

Piecing curves is one of those challenges that some quilters can't resist. A curved seam presents us with many problems due to grain line and bias. This is the reason why so many quilts with curves and waves are not pieced, but appliquéd by turning the curved edge under.

It is possible, however, to piece a curved seam with minimal effort and excellent results. All you need is a little time, patience, and careful, steady hands.

In this demonstration, I'm piecing a simple curved block and the pieces were cut from Marti Michelle's Large Drunkard's Path template set.

However, it's good to remember that you can find drunkard's path fabric dies from AccuQuilt Go as well. Again, this is a quicker way to cut the pieces, but so long as you take the time to prepare the die with marks to line the fabric up on grain, this method is still an extremely accurate way to cut this shape.

Cutting Instructions:

Cut 6 inch square of Fabric A - Cut this shape using the "L" shape template.

Cut 6 inch square of fabric B - Cut this shape using the "Pie" shape template

Piecing Instructions:

1. The Drunkards Path block is created using an "L" shape and a pie shape. Fold both shapes in half, marking the center line with a crease.

2. Lay the pie shaped piece over the "L" shape with right sides together, lining up the crease line. Place a pin here, holding both pieces together right at the midpoint.

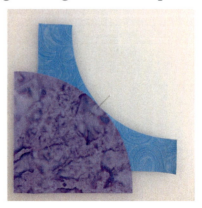

Curved Seam Piecing Instructions continued

3. Very carefully pin the edges of the seam as well, being careful not to pull and distort the blocks. Yes, the "L" shape will have enough give for the pie shape to fit properly.

4. Using a scrap charger, start piecing the shapes together, double checking that you're using a perfect ¼-inch seam allowance.

5. Continue stitching to the center of the block, pausing occasionally to ease the pie shape into the "L" shape very carefully.

You can see the locations of my fingers in the photo on the right gently pressing the block together.

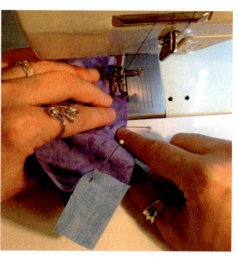

7. Stitch to the end, again being careful to stay exactly in the seam allowance. Remove the block from your machine and it will look like this:

8. The seam will have plenty of ease, if this block was created correctly. This means that you can press the seam allowance in either direction. Yes, you can even press this curved seam OPEN!

Piecing Project - Drunkard's Path Quilt

Stitch many curved seam blocks from page 110 and arrange them in this seemingly random way to create a Drunkard's Path quilt. As you can see, it doesn't matter if your curved seams are perfect. In this design, curves don't match up to create circles, which could be eye-catching if pieced inaccurately. This random arrangement will allow you plenty of stress-free practice on curved seam piecing.

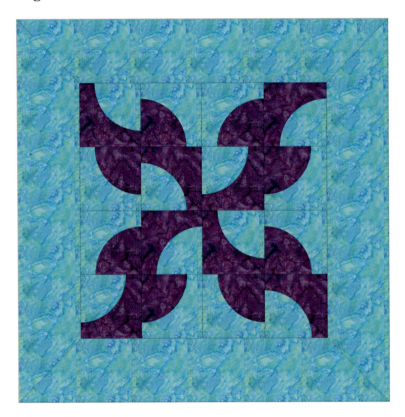

Material List:

2/3 yard Fabric A (Purple)

1 ½ yard Fabric B (Blue)

Cotton thread to match Fabric B

Fabric Cutting Chart

Fabric A	1 - 5 ½ inch width-of-fabric strip cut into 8 pie shapes
	2 - 6 ½ inch width-of-fabric strips cut into 8 "L" shapes
From Fabric B:	1 - 5 ½ inch width-of-fabric strip cut into 8 pie shapes
	2 - 6 ½ inch width-of-fabric strips cut into 8 "L" shapes
	4 - 6 ½ inch width-of-fabric strips for the borders

Drunkard's Path Quilt Piecing Instructions

1. Cut and arrange the pieces by color and shape. Pin the Fabric A pie shapes to the Fabric B "L" shapes and piece each seam following the directions on page 110.

2. Repeat with the Fabric B pie shapes and the Fabric A "L" shapes. You should now have 16 curved blocks pieced.

3. Piece the curved squares together into rows. Gently finger press seams open, then press to flatten with a hot, dry iron.

4. Piece the rows together, carefully matching the seam lines of every square. Gently finger press the seams open, then press to flatten with a hot, dry iron.

5. This large Drunkard's Path block will now measure 24 ½-inches square. Expand the size of this quilt top and challenge yourself to stitch this quilt up a notch by adding mitered borders!

Review piecing a mitered border on page 82.

Curved Seam Piecing Tips

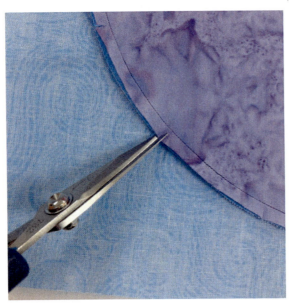

- Always find the midpoint of the seam first, and pin securely.

- Make sure to start with a perfect ¼-inch seam allowance. Starting the seam can be the trickiest part of curved seam piecing.

- Maintain a perfect ¼-inch seam allowance throughout your seam.

- Carefully handle your block so it doesn't distort.

- Clip seams only as necessary. If you're cutting from well-designed templates, you shouldn't need to clip very much.

- When all else fails, trim the edges of the block down to a set size after it's pieced to ensure that all the curves will match perfectly.

Trouble Shooting Curved Seams

Ungainly Wobbles

Don't fret if your curved seam resembles a toddler on shaky legs. This seam was stitched fairly haphazardly, sometimes inside, sometimes outside the seam allowance, which led to a very wobbly curve.

Start your seam properly and maintain that crucial ¼ inch seam allowance throughout by continually stopping and shifting the L shaped and curved shape pieces to ease the fabrics together.

Hello Ms. Pleaty

Yes, pleats are a common side effect of piecing curves. This is a perfectly normal issue to struggle with, and it also has two simple fixes:

1. Double starch your fabric before cutting your shapes

2. Stop often to ease the two fabrics together evenly.

The stiffer the fabric, the less these off-grain fabrics are going to shift on you, and the more often you stop to ease, the less excess fabric you will have to potentially pleat.

~ Chapter 11 ~
Paper Piecing for Perfection

With so much knowledge under your belt and skills built through our many practice projects, it's now time to divulge a little secret:

There is a way to piece perfectly and never stitch a single perfect seam allowance, or pin to match seam lines.

It's called paper piecing and we actually piece on paper. The block design is laid out on paper and you stitch on the lines in a systematic way to piece each shape.

Paper piecing patterns can range from super simple to extremely complex, and it's a neat way to produce perfect sharp points and angles that might be very challenging to piece in the traditional way.

But as with all things in quilting – there's no way to save time! Paper piecing might be a short cut to perfection, but it's definitely a lot more time consuming than regular piecing.

Chapter 11 Sections:

Paper Piecing Overview - Page 116

Paper Pieced Boat Block - Page 117

Paper Pieced Ship's Star Block - Page 119

Boat Block Pattern - Page 122

Ship's Star Block Pattern - 123

Paper Piecing Overview

The idea behind paper piecing, or foundation piecing, is simple: rather than create a block by stitching pieces together, you stitch pieces onto a foundation of paper or fabric.

The pieces are stitched on one at a time and flipped over so that all the edges finish just as smooth and perfect as they do with regular piecing. If you stitch onto paper, the paper is torn away in the final stage leaving just the fabric block behind.

By using a foundation for your pieces, you don't need to worry about cutting your pieces precisely. **You don't even have to worry about grain line.**

In fact, paper piecing is a great way to use up your stash of fabric scraps and odds and ends. Paper pieced blocks can finish as big or as small as you want, depending on the size of your foundation design.

You can also piece together multiple foundations to create larger blocks. Almost any design - flowers, animals, even words - can be pieced precisely using paper piecing.

Paper piecing can help you produce perfectly crisp, sharp points, matching seams, and intricate shapes, all without fussing with precise cutting or templates.

A big downside to paper piecing is that it is very time consuming. Each piece must be added one at a time, trimmed and pressed before moving on to the next piece.

Another downside is the seam allowances are pressed to one side, which could cause a darker color fabric to show through a lighter color. Be mindful of this when selecting your colors and trimming.

When it comes time to quilt a quilt top created with paper piecing, you will need to be mindful of the seam allowances. Thicker spots where multiple seams come together can be tricky to quilt over in free motion.

Despite these downsides, paper piecing remains a tried and true method for producing perfectly matched seams and crisp, sharp triangle points.

Reversed note: Because the fabric is stitched and flipped on one side, and the lines you stitch along are on the opposite side, your paper pieced patterns will always be reversed from the completed block design.

Paper Piecing a Boat Block

This cute paper pieced boat block is a simple design that will allow you to practice all the steps to paper piecing on one paper pattern. Copy the pattern on page 122 and then enjoy the instant gratification of being able to easily piece the block perfectly by stitching on marked lines.

Materials for Boat Block:

Fabric scraps for the boat, water, sky, and boat flag

Piecing Instructions:

1. Copy your pattern and double check it is printed the correct size. The outer square should measure 6 ½ inches. Also make sure to lower your stitch length to 1.5 mm.

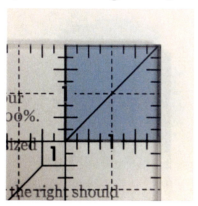

You can double check that a piece fills the space completely by holding the paper up to the light.

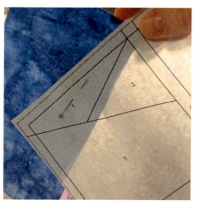

2. Start with piece #1, a sky piece. Lay it on the back side of the paper, make sure it completely fills the #1 spot, then pin it in place.

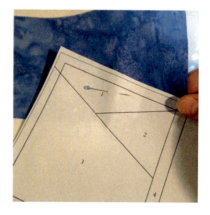

3. Next place a flag colored scrap on piece #2 so it fills that space completely. Flip it and align the edge with piece #1.

Paper Piecing Boat Block Instructions continued

4. Flip the paper over and stitch the seam from the top along the line on the paper between piece #1 and #2.

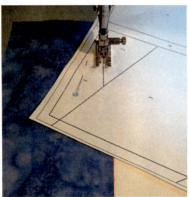

5. Trim the excess fabric beyond the seam to ¼ inch. Fold piece #2 over to cover its space and press to flatten it in place.

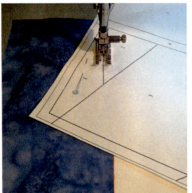

6. Move on to piece #3 - another sky piece. Make sure your fabric scrap is big enough to fully cover the piece.

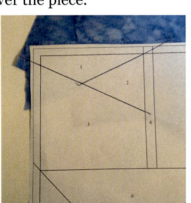

7. Repeat the steps to flip the piece over and stitch on the line between piece #2 and #3.

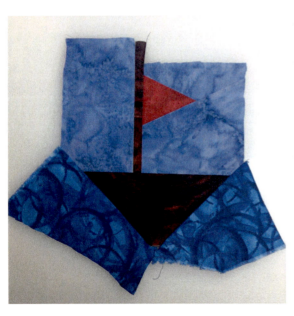

Continue to add pieces according to the numbers on the pattern. Make sure to always trim down the seam allowance behind each shape before adding the next piece.

Slowly your boat block will start to appear, on the opposite side of the printed paper.

Once all the pieces have been pieced in place, cover the right side of the block with a pressing cloth and give your block a final press.

Flip the block over and using the outer paper line as a guide, trim it down to 6 ½ inches.

Carefully pull the paper away from the back. Be very gentle and try not to tug excessively on the stitches as you pull the paper away.

Paper Piecing Ship's Star Block

Many paper pieced blocks can be pieced using one sheet of paper, or foundation, as we learned with the boat block on page 117.

But many more paper pieced blocks must be first pieced in sections, then those sections connected together using the same perfect piecing techniques we've learned throughout this book.

In situations like these just remember all the steps we've learned in previous chapters on piecing precisely and you'll be fine.

Materials for Ship's Star Block:

Fabric scraps of the following colors: Red, White, Blue

Piecing Instructions:

1. Copy and print the pattern on page 123 and double check it's printed the correct size by checking the 1-inch square in the corner. Also make sure to lower your stitch length to 1.5 mm which will make the paper easier to tear away.

Finally, cut the squares apart through the space in the middle to create four small squares.

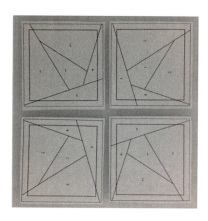

2. Start with piece #1 - white star point. Place piece #2 (blue background) on top, then flip over and check that both fabric edges extend beyond the stitching line.

3. Pin the pieces in place from the paper side if needed. Flip the paper over and stitch along the line between piece #1 and #2.

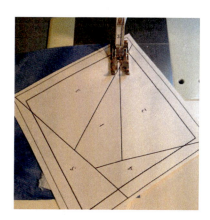

Paper Piecing Ship's Star Block Instructions continued

4. Flip to the fabric side and carefully trim any excess seam allowance down to ¼ inch.

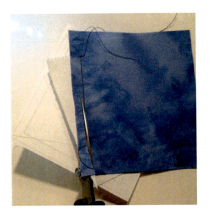

5. Repeat the same steps with piece #3 - another blue background piece. Press the block after each seam to flatten the layers.

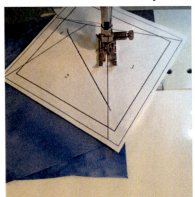

6. Next add piece #4 - a red star point. Follow with piece #5, also in red.

7. Flip to the paper side and trim the square to 3 ½ inches using the printed lines as a guide.

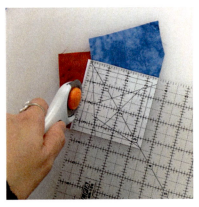

8. Repeat these steps with the three remaining paper patterns. You should now have four pieced sections.

9. Remove the paper gently from all four pieces. Be careful not to distort the seams as each piece is cut exactly the correct size.

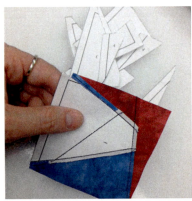

Paper Piecing Ship's Star Block Instructions continued

11. Piece two sets of these units together, matching the star points. Watch out for bulky areas where multiple fabric layers can pull out of shape as you piece. Press the seams open carefully.

12. Piece the two halves of the block together, matching the middle seam and star points. Finger press the seam allowance open, then give the block a final press and measure it to check the size. This block should now measure 6 ½ inches exactly and have perfectly matching, beautiful points.

Now that you've learned paper piecing, please don't throw away everything you've learned about regular piecing. Yes, paper piecing makes piecing complicated blocks with many triangle points much easier, but it is more time consuming than regular piecing.

Quick Strip Paper Piecing Class

What if you could combine the speed of strip piecing with the easy precision of paper piecing?

Peggy Martin has created a method that combines these two techniques and has taught it in the Craftsy class **Quick Strip Paper Piecing.**

In this class you will learn how to paper piece multiple quilts very quickly using long strips. This combination of strip piecing and paper piecing is amazingly fast and accurate, and the projects for this class are simple and fun.

Learn more about Quick Strip Paper Piecing at Craftsy.com

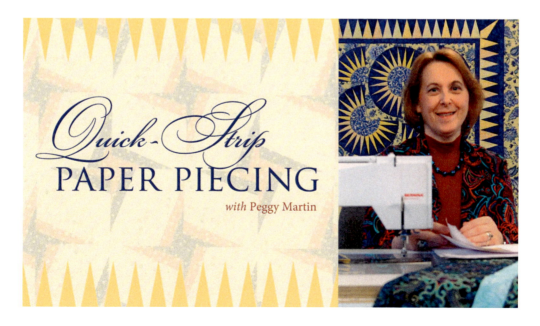

Boat Block Pattern

Directions: Copy this page with no scaling or enlargement. Please feel free to make as many copies as you like. You will need one printed sheet for every block you wish to piece.

After printing the copy, measure the 1 inch square in the corner to check the page has printed properly with no distortion.

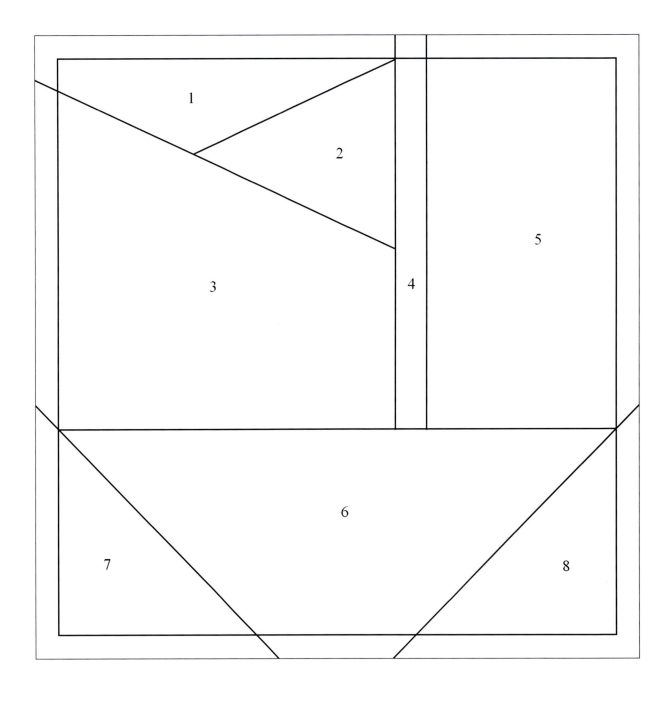

Ship's Star Block Pattern

Directions: Copy this page with no scaling or enlargement. Please feel free to make as many copies as you like. You will need one printed sheet for every block you wish to piece.

After printing the copy, measure the 1 inch square in the corner to check the page has printed properly with no distortion.

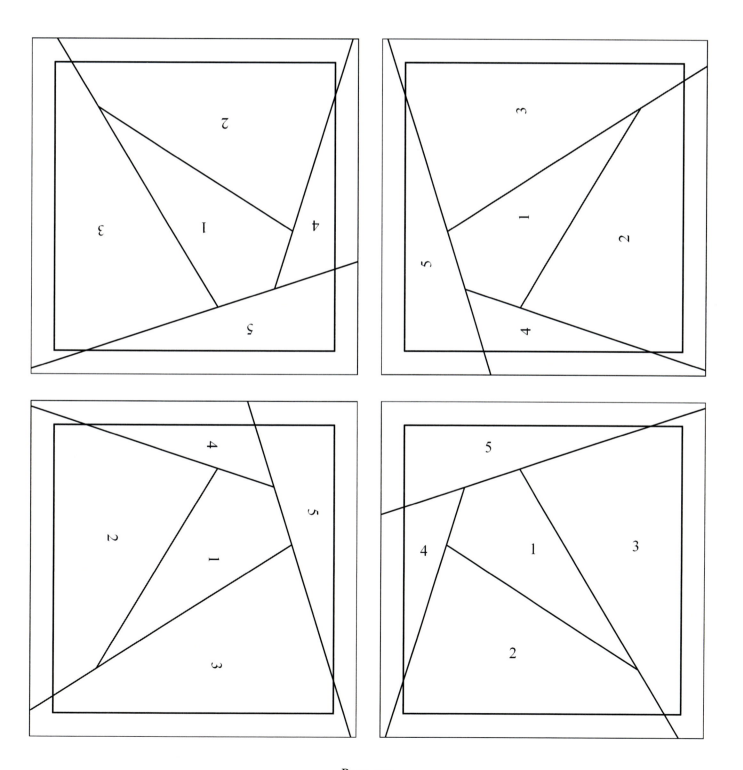

Conclusion

Are you ready to start piecing perfectly?

By now you have the skills to piece almost any block you can imagine. All you need to do is start using the steps in this book in the quilts you are making right now.

As you can probably tell, there is no single master trick to perfect piecing. This is a step-by-step, methodical process of preparing, cutting, and piecing fabrics together, and yes, it may be very different from the way you construct quilts right now.

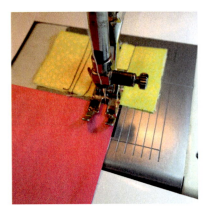

When trying out these new methods, pay attention to the different ways your fabrics feel during cutting and piecing. Compare your old way of measuring and cutting with the methods in this book.

What I hope you've learned in this book is the WHY behind every seam. If your seams don't match or your fabrics feel out of control, I hope you understand why that's happening and what you can do about it. Just knowing what is really happening to your fabrics and taking the mystery out of the process will be enough to shed light on issues you may have struggled with for years.

I also hope that you will begin using all of these tips and tricks to end the unpredictability in your fabric. It's such a comforting feeling of skill and knowledge to be able to piece a complicated block and trust that all the seams will match perfectly.

No, there is not a single step, a perfect tool, or single golden rule to perfect piecing. Instead it is the combination of many steps, meticulous attention to detail, and patience that creates a perfectly pieced quilt.

You now have the knowledge of how this process works, how fabric behaves, and how to build habits into your piecing experience that will make many steps an easy addition to your day. Give these new ideas a try on the basic skill building quilts in this book and you will see an amazing difference in every seam you piece.

Let's go quilt!

Leah Day

BUILD SKILLS WITH THE BUILDING BLOCKS QUILT

Are you ready to put your piecing skills to the test? Now is the time to build upon the lessons you've learned by piecing the 42 blocks of this beautiful skill-building sampler quilt.

In the Building Blocks Quilt Pattern, you will hone your skills piecing fun, traditional blocks like Pinwheel, Home Sweet Home, Bountiful Baskets, and Sawtooth Star. You'll also expand your abilities with a few unconventionally pieced modern blocks as well.

Best of all - this pattern is not just about piecing! Each block comes with a full-sized quilting guide so you can mark your block and free motion quilt it easily on your home machine.

Bonus! Watch how to piece and free motion quilt every block in this quilt in free videos created by Leah and Josh Day

Each block is quilted separately so the project will be manageable no matter how small your sewing machine. You'll also find detailed connection instructions so you can bind the blocks together to finish your Building Blocks Quilt.

Save $10 on the Building Blocks Quilt Pattern

Use coupon code: **perfect10**

Find this pattern at LeahDay.com

Made in the USA
Middletown, DE
17 October 2014